HE LAUGHS AT FEAR

He Laughs At Fear

ISBN: 978-1-60920-009-1
Printed in the United States of America
©2010 by Patty Johnson
All rights reserved

Cover and interior design by Isaac Publishing, Inc.

Library of Congress Cataloging-in-Publication Data

Unless otherwise noted, all Scripture quotations are from the Hebrew
Greek Study Bible, NIV 1996
(Chatanooga, TN: AMG Publishers, 1996)

Isaac Publishing, Inc.
P.O. 342
Three Rivers, MI 49093
www.isaacpublishing.com

Please direct your inquiries to admin@isaacpublishing.com

ENDORSEMENTS

"When a person shares their challenges of life and the victories obtained through faith in God, it is an encouragement for all. Such is this book by Patty Johnson. You will be encouraged and inspired as you face your trials in life and your expectancy for victory after victory will increase."

Janet McGee,
U.S. Regional Director
Aglow International

"It gives me great pleasure to endorse Patty's inspired work. In the time I have known her I have found Patty to be stirring, humorous and incredibly talented. She has an amazing ability to communicate the deep and profound things of the Spirit which come out of a very real relationship with the Lord."

Rev. Michael Whitman
Pastor, International Minister, Missionary

"I met Patty Johnson several times at various conferences throughout the years. My first impression of Patty was a woman who was very content in staying in the background. She seemed to be very introspective, gentle, and when I looked into her eyes, I knew instinctively that there was more to her than what others painted her to be.

In 2007, I asked Patty to accompany me on a short mission trip to Hungary. The only observation at that time for me was being obedient to the voice of God when He told me to take Patty with me. I did. To my surprise, I was stunned when she began to minister the word. I knew why God asked me to have her accompany me on this trip. The power of God's anointing was on her. Her ability to extract the simple things in life was worth noting, and I was able then, to see why many people assume the wrong things about her. The people of Hungary were blessed by her authentic presence and compassion that she had for them. It was in that year that I decided to have Patty come with me to other nations. I thank God for the privilege of knowing Patty. She is the genuine package that people need to witness to know that God is real. Simplicity and humility are her virtues. You will see this young generation rising up calling Patty Johnson a true woman of God.

What I like about Patty is her willingness to share the broken pieces of her life to others so that they can experience the same impartation of God's healing and restoration. Very few women that I have met in my life possess the virtue of transparency as seen in Patty. For those who are self-seeking and lack authenticity, Patty's character, transparency, and integrity will certainly disarm them.

This book that Patty Johnson has written about her life is a testimony of God's grace and love for a woman who, by the world's standards, would have been a statistical failure. God saw another plan for her life. Every human story is precious and has meaning in the sight of God. Patty is the only one who can tell her story to the world about the twists and turns in her life of rejection. Yet, in the midst of finding resolve in God, now it is Patty's turn to participate in the Divine plan of sparing other broken lives."

Cheryll A. Bellamy
Attorney at Law

"I don't remember the exact date and I suppose that's not overly important, but I do know that it was a long dark mark on the spiritual timeline of my life when I met Patty Johnson. Lines of that import mean that a significant or momentous change took place and something triggered that change. Patty was that catalyst! I have been inspired, encouraged, challenged, prayed for, ministered to, revealed(!), and loved. Patty's courage and perseverance, her spirit of the overcomer and deep passion and zeal for the Lord, her total and sometimes gut-wrenching honesty, tears and contagious laughter will draw you to her like a spiritual magnet as it has for me. Her deep longing for the things of the Lord, for Himself alone, has constantly called me to a higher level of intimacy with Him! She definitely will not allow me to 'stay put!' (for which I'm thankful!)

As you soak up the powerful words of this book, I promise you, you'll be drawn into the picture Patty vividly portrays of her life and testimony. You will not only aspire to, but will know that you are being called by God to His higher purposes for your life and that He will be faithful to bring it to fruition. I know because I am His work in progress and God has used this special author to aid in the fruit-bearing. Alleluia and Amen!"

Connie Siefker
Northwest Ohio Area President
Aglow International

"This is a story of God's faithfulness in difficult circumstances as He molds and transforms each of us in His likeness."

Paula Bryson
Ohio State Prayer Coordinator
Aglow International

Acknowledgements

My heart overflows in thanksgiving for those whose lives have been inseparably and eternally interwoven with mine. In all the memories of my journey, your faces are there. Your love, your voices, your laughter have forged my story. To you, my family, I dedicate this book. I honor my husband Hollis who has been to me a rock of strength and who has greatly exhorted me to write this book. To my four children, you are the joy of my heart. I love you ... forever.

To Esther Woodworth, I thank you for investing in me all those years ago. Your friendship and the testimony of your life brought me to the cross, where I found purpose and eternal life.

I especially acknowledge and thank my dear friend Mary Whitmire. When I walked through the valley of the shadow of death, you never deserted me. Your tender mercy and compassion brought me forth into the light and your arms of love carried me into my promised land.

And what is to be said of my cheering squad - my special friends without whom I do not believe this book would ever have been written? I so clearly remember Carol's email that long-ago morning: " ...maybe you will write a book, Patty." You believed in me and spurred me on. To Carol Foulkes, Connie Siefker, Mary Lou Stechschulte, Judy Blankemeyer, and Cheryll Bellamy, thank you with all my heart! You gave me courage.

Patty Johnson
Summer 2010

HE LAUGHS AT FEAR

Patty Johnson

Isaac Publishing, Inc.
www.isaacpublishing.com
1.888.273.4569
PO. Box 342
Three Rivers, MI 49093

Introduction

In her book *Prodigals and Those Who Love Them*, Ruth Bell Graham shares the following poem:

Perhaps
she will land
upon That Shore,
not in full sail
but rather,
a bit of broken wreckage
for Him
to gather.

Perhaps
He walks Those Shores
seeking such,
who have believed
a little,
suffered much
and so,
been washed Ashore.

Perhaps
of all the souls redeemed
they most
adore.

---London, 1972[1]

This is a book about fear. It is a book about the power to overcome fear. It is the story of the transformation that takes place in a life when it is picked up and held in the arms of the One who created it. Fear comes in all colors and all decibel levels. This book will usher you into your Father's heart of love where you will touch and experience that place of overshadowing security in Him. It is there that you will be empowered to overcome all fear.

The truths in this book apply to every life, as there are few who have never experienced some measure of fear. And yet, in Father's heart, there are those for whom this book is most especially written. It is the ones of whom Ruth Graham has written in her poem above. Those whose lives have never been in full sail. Those ones who have suffered much, and often, without notice, been washed Ashore as a bit of broken wreckage.

Your heavenly Papa knows who you are. For long years you have lived in the shadow of darkness where peace has eluded you. You cannot remember a day that you did not wake up to the weight of a wall of fear closing in around you. Weariness. Hopelessness. Defeat. Some of you have been abused. Some of you have abused yourself. Some feel shame. Some feel rage. Some feel paralyzed, hunted down, on the run, trapped like an animal. You thought that you had long ago stopped searching the horizon for the goodness of life. And yet, dearly beloved, your hand reached for this book.

> *Can plunder be taken from warriors,*
> *or captives rescued from the fierce?*
> *But this is what the Lord says:*
> *"Yes, captives will be taken from warriors,*
> *and plunder retrieved from the fierce;*
> *I will contend with those who contend with you,"*
>   *—Isaiah 49:24, 25*

The Lord Jesus Christ comes as our Liberator. He walks Those Shores seeking such as you. He comes to gather you near to His heart, to sing over you as He holds you close, to contend for you, and to rescue you from the fierce warriors who have held you captive. The message of this book comes as a shaft of light shining down into your dungeon. It is the voice of the Lord that breaks the cedars… that strikes with flashes of lightning…that twists the oaks and strips the forests bare. Psalm 29:5-9 Look up, dear reader. There is nowhere that His voice cannot reach. It is His voice that has come to deliver you from all fear.

Most names in this book have been changed.

CONTENTS

Do you give the horse his strength
or clothe his neck with a flowing mane?
Do you make him leap like a locust,
striking terror with his proud snorting?
He paws fiercely, rejoicing in his strength,
and charges into the fray.
HE LAUGHS AT FEAR *afraid of nothing,*
he does not shy away from the sword.
The quiver rattles against his side,
along with the flashing spear and lance.
In frenzied excitement he eats up the ground;
he cannot stand still when the trumpet sounds.
At the blast of the trumpet he snorts, "Aha!"
he catches the scent of battle from afar,
the shout of commanders and the battle cry.

—Job 39:19-25

CHAPTER ONE

A Closet Full of Gowns

I woke up that morning full of wonder as the dream danced inside my heart. Magic seemed to linger in the air and I felt almost giddy. Over and over I rehearsed the unusual dream, captivated by what it might possibly mean. I poured my first fresh cup of coffee, found my journal, and began to write.

The House

In my dream my husband and I were standing together inside a house that we had just purchased. The house was old and smaller than what we would have liked for it to be. But we didn't mind. We knew that we were in God's will and that we would be able to adjust to anything. As I looked around, I thought of some things that we could do to change the house and make it better. But then I was aware of permanent structural components that had been set in place by the builder of the house and that could not be altered.

The kitchen in the house was very unusual. It was equipped to be used commercially. There were huge vats of oil for preparing large quantities of food. At one end of the kitchen, set apart and enclosed in beautiful lattice work, was a little white garden table and two small chairs. Standing there, I thought of our four children. They were not with us, but in the dream I knew that in time they would be coming to live there.

Upstairs

Suddenly I was upstairs in a part of the house that was all new.

The rooms there were larger than any rooms I'd ever been in. They were very spacious and filled with light that seemed to be alive. The carpeting and the woodwork were all new. The rooms were empty and I was there alone. I had never been in these rooms before and I couldn't believe that they had come with the house. I knew the room I was standing in was our bedroom, yet I also understood it was much more than that. The room continued on and on beyond what I could see. It was as though it became one with open space, enlarging as it went and rolling right into heaven.

Several walls in the room were lined with sturdy, well-built closets. In my dream I approached one of them and opened it. Inside there hung several floor-length gowns, each one elegant and richly jeweled. I knew the gowns belonged to the woman who had moved out and that quite likely she had forgotten them, yet I was excited that she had forgotten them. Then I observed that they were all size 10 and would be too large for me to wear. As I was pondering this, I saw that one of the gowns was smaller and knew that it would fit me perfectly. I pulled it out and realized that it had been intentionally designed to be a very small size 10. The price tag read $777.

All at once the woman who had lived in the house before, and who owned all the gowns, was standing in the room with her four young children. I thought that she had come to take the dresses, and although I was disappointed, I knew that it was right. She sat down on a large bed while I stood somewhat to the back of her and continued to look directly at her. Then I woke up.

The Master Builder

In her book, *Dream Language*, co-authored with her husband James, Michal Ann Goll writes:

> *Dreams can lead us to the heart of the Father. You can receive the most awesome dream, record it in your journal, and even spend hours pondering its meaning, but if it does not draw you closer to the Lord, you have missed the most important point of all.*

Dream language awakens your heart and activates childlike faith where you know that with God anything is possible. Dream big dreams! Let these God-sized dreams explode out of you and affect virtually every area of your life.[2]

Dreams are a language of the heart. They are one of the ways that heaven communicates with us. Dan 2:28 says: there is a God in heaven who reveals mysteries. And so, when we are asleep, our Father pulls back the veil and paints a picture, tells a story, sings a song, or even takes us on a journey, all through dream language. God wants to enlarge our capacity to believe. He wants to teach and instruct us, comfort and encourage us, sometimes even give us direction or warning. Sometimes He simply wants to share His secrets with us. Like all that He does, the dreams that He sends are not without purpose. He whispers His love over us as He invites us to come closer. He delights in us and says, "Listen to my heart… let your heart be awakened to the wonder of who I AM… receive fresh understanding."

In many ways the dream that I received that early morning long ago was an invitation from heaven. There are eternal truths revealed in this dream that impart God's heart for each one of his sons and daughters. The dream came at a time in my life when I was emerging out of a long season of darkness. The sun was just beginning to shine for me again and I was not sure if I could trust it. God knew my fragileness. And in His tender Fatherly way, His voice was calling to me through the dream, "Yes! Yes! My little one. All is well." It was an invitation to put my hand in His and trust Him with my future.

In Mt 7:24, 26 Jesus speaks about a wise man who built his house on the rock and a foolish man who built his house on sand. We know that each man's house represents his life. In my dream the house represents my life. I can remember going up the pretty walkway and entering the house with great anticipation. My expectations ran high. Yet as Hollis and I stood there in the downstairs, I was confronted with reality. Everything in the house was much older and smaller than I had thought it would be.

It is not unusual in this journey of life for reality to be outsized by the longings in our soul. We each carry around a big suitcase full of bright and shiny dreams until it seems our arm becomes glued to the handle. As I surveyed these downstairs rooms in my dream, my imagination began to visualize things I could "do" so that the house could more closely resemble the blueprints in my suitcase. But God, the *builder of everything* (Heb 3:4), had wisely and lovingly set in place all the details of the house with me in mind. Some things would never be mine to choose.

We are created in our Father's image and we are dreamers because we carry His nature. He is The Dreamer and The Keeper of Dreams. All dreams begin and end in Him. The dreams that He dreams over our life are the same bright and shiny, albeit somewhat askew, dreams that we carry in our suitcase. They originated in His heart and it is His Hand that put them into our heart. The peace that I felt in my dream was a proud Papa's way of revealing to me that although I still knew every tiny detail of my own set of blueprints, in the depths of my heart I had truly surrendered the suitcase to Him. He deeply wanted me to know that He was moved by this display of undivided trust within my spirit. I knew the house was His choice for me. And that was sufficient. His road to our dreams often takes a different path.

There was much the Lord showed me about the kitchen in this house. The kitchen is a place where family, friends and guests gather... a place where nourishment is served up. This kitchen was a commercial one, which speaks of quantities large enough to feed crowds. Jesus is painting a picture of a glorious kingdom truth. Jer 29:11 says, "For I know the plans I have for you," declares the Lord, "plans to prosper you and not to harm you, plans to give you hope and a future." The Lord's plan is that great provision should flow through each of our lives so that we will be a place of feeding, a place of nourishment, for all who hunger.

This kitchen contained huge vats of oil. Oil is rich in symbolism.

It speaks of Jesus who is called Christos, the anointed One. It speaks of the presence of the Holy Spirit and the power to heal and restore the broken. In Lk 10:34, when the Samaritan came upon the man who had been stripped of his clothes, beaten, and left half dead, he took pity on him, went to him and bandaged his wounds, and poured on oil and wine. Oh the glory and the wonder of our great King! He lifts the burden of the suitcase from off our shoulder, breathes His resurrection life upon our broken dreams, and turns them into an unending supply of rich, heavenly oil, to be poured out upon those lives that have been stripped, beaten, and wounded.

The last thing I saw in this kitchen, set apart from the work area and enclosed in intricate lattice work, was the little secluded garden table for two. The Holy Spirit is painting another picture. It is the Song of Songs 2:8-10:

> *Listen! My LOVER!*
> *Look! Here he comes, leaping across the mountains,*
> *bounding over the hills. My Lover is like a gazelle or a young*
> *stag. Look! There he stands behind our wall,*
> *gazing through the windows, peering through the lattice.*
> *My Lover spoke and said to me, "Arise, my darling,*
> *my beautiful one, and come with me."*

These words are the heart's song of all those entrusted to steward the golden oil. Always they are crying out to others, "Listen! Look! Here he comes... leaping... bounding... Look! There he stands... gazing... peering." He is their Lover and they are His beautiful ones. They arise and go with Him. It is a relationship of intimate romance. The lattice work speaks of the hidden, secret place of their love, far away from the crowds. It speaks of the bridal veil, where only those who come close can see through... only those who have built an altar to Him. The prophet Zechariah calls them sons of fresh oil. The oil they dispense from their vats is fresh and living because of the little table for two where they lavish their love and worship upon the Anointed One… where they become those whom He calls His friends.

When the Lord took me to the upstairs of the house, I was by myself. The rooms were a very great surprise to me as I had never seen them before and did not know they were part of the house. There was quite a sense of adventure and discovery. The light was bright, clean, and vibrant. Everything was new and fresh and large. In the dream I was exhilarated and silly with joy. The windows and the walls seemed to be as one with the heavens. I knew that if I walked forever I would still not reach the end of the rooms.

This was my future. God was showing me my future. Jesus was upgrading my spiritual eyesight and taking me inside His heart to see His dreams and plans for my life. Jesus says in Mt 6:6, "When you pray, go into your room [closet], close the door and pray to your Father, who is unseen. Then your Father, who sees what is done in secret, will reward you." The closets in the upstairs room are a picture of our prayer life. The elegant, richly jeweled gowns represent the giftings and the callings that God desires to clothe us in. Although they exist in the Father's heart long before He forms us in our mother's womb, it is through our prayers that they are birthed into the earth realm.

Many of those things that God has prepared for us are as yet too large for us and so are kept ready, awaiting our maturity. Yet Jesus beams with delight as He treats us to a sneak prevue. His voice, strong and confident, awakens the stirrings of hope within us.

> *Come see what is in My heart for you. Come see what I have planned for you. That is why I brought you upstairs. That is why I brought you here to these rooms. Come see where I am taking you in days ahead. I know you are not yet ready, but I am not concerned. I am preparing you. You need not fear. I am enlarging your heart, enlarging your courage, enlarging your trust in Me. I am pouring my love into you and restoring you and once again you will sing as in the days of your youth. So*

come here as often as you wish. I have given you these rooms.
[Somehow I understood that the little garden table for two
was the secret passageway to the rooms upstairs.] *And in
days to come, I shall indeed clothe you in gowns fashioned for
royalty.*

In my dream the gowns were beautiful to me. I was deeply
drawn to them and desired them with all my heart. I was absolutely
delighted that one of them was small enough to fit me right away.
And I knew the Father had given His undivided, detailed attention
to this dress.

Immersed in the gowns in the dream, I quite forgot the sense
that I was in somebody else's closet. Then quite abruptly I saw the
woman who had suddenly appeared in the room with her four young
children. I knew she was the woman who had lived in the house
before and I knew that it was only right that she should take the
gowns. Yet my heart ached with disappointment. Instead she sat
down on a large bed that had not been there before. And as I stood
there to the back of her, quietly looking at her, I began to realize that
she was me.

This place that we were in was my future. And she was the
old me. She was the woman who had lived in the older, smaller
downstairs. She was the woman who had journeyed through the
long season of testing, surrendering her suitcase to the Keeper of
Dreams, and building a future through her tears, her prayers, her
faith and perseverance. She was the one who had birthed this room
and the beautiful jeweled gowns.

BUT HOW HAD SHE GOTTEN HERE
AND WHAT DID IT MEAN?

CHAPTER TWO

Under New Management

The nurse's hand rested firmly on my abdomen as Dr. Davis tended to our tiny newborn son, just moments old. Her words were barely audible. "There's another one, isn't there, Dr. Davis?" she inquired. Four minutes later, to the surprise and delight of all, our second little son was delivered. A thousand gaily colored balloons floated down from heaven and filled my heart.

Apprehended

Our first daughter, Melissa, was just a toddler when her daddy came home from combat duty in Vietnam. We were so young and eager to be a family again. We settled happily into military life at Fort Ord, California, where the Pacific Ocean basked just outside our window. The year passed quickly, and soon we were packing up the car for the long trip east to Ohio where Hollis would begin his career in the corporate business world. This time there were two little girls traveling with us!

Hollis and I had both grown up attending church. But in those first years of our marriage, moving from one military base to another, one town to another, absorbed in ourselves, it seemed so much easier to just sleep in on Sunday mornings. But now we were aware that our little girls were growing and we found ourselves thinking a lot about wanting to be part of a church. So we searched until we found one that felt right. And it was there that I met Esther.

Esther was nine years older than me. She taught history at the local high-school and was the mother of two young boys in grade school. There was no natural reason for her to be drawn to a stay-at-home mom of two very little girls. Yet she extended to me a friendship beyond anything I had ever known. She quite loved me. And I'd never known that kind of love. Everything about Esther was different. She seemed to glow. She knew Jesus and she talked about Him with a very natural and personal affection that was all new to me. I would watch her and think longingly to myself, *How wonderful to have God choose you like that. I wish He'd choose me.* But I was sure He never would.

In time, I became pregnant again and I so wanted a boy. Esther would tell me over and over to pray. I said, "Esther, the baby is already IN there! Why should I pray?" But she would say, "Pray, Patty. God can do anything." I wasn't sure how to even do it. But for months I prayed. I prayed as I ran the vacuum cleaner. I prayed when I did the dishes. Over and over, all spring and all summer long, I prayed and asked God for a son.

October arrived and labor set in. Hollis and I were at the hospital when just past midnight Esther surprised us in the delivery room. Dressed in a long white medical gown and face mask, she seemed to be an angel. There, together with Hollis and me, she watched as God un-wrapped His well-kept secret and heaven poured out its double blessing. Not one boy, but two! Not one son, but two!

We moved frequently with Hollis' career in those early years and it was not long before the moving van came and packed up our growing family. Soon I was far away from Esther and I missed her. Her words and her love echoed in my heart. In the spring her family came and stayed with us for a week. Oh, how I wanted to know the Lord like she did and oh how many questions I had saved up!

Our days together flew by and soon her entire family was all piling into their car for their long trip home. We stood in our driveway hugging good-bye in the early morning darkness. The air was cold. I was aching at letting her go… She was the only link to something I was so afraid I might never find… Something my heart was so hungry for. But she knew. She knew. And she handed me a piece of paper with the title of a book written on it. "I want you to read this," she said.

Sealed

I woke all the children up early, got Melissa off to kindergarten, strapped the other three into their car-seats, and headed to the bookstore, arriving before it opened! I bought the book, *9 O'Clock in the Morning*, by Father Dennis Bennett and I took it home and devoured it. I was cooking spaghetti and meatballs that day and I remember stirring the sauce with one hand and holding the book in the other hand while I read.

As soon as every little head was in bed for the night, I went downstairs to our basement where I could be alone. At midnight I finished Father Bennett's book. Everything was stirring inside me. Slipping down onto the floor, I stretched myself out face-down on the bright orange carpet, and prayed the first real prayer of my life. After all these years, I remember it just as I spoke it: "Lord Jesus, I don't know you like the man in that book. And Lord Jesus, I don't love you like the man in that book. But Lord Jesus, I want that. Teach me how to love you. And teach me how to live my life for you. I want everything that you have for me."

I was 28 years old. But in many ways my life had only just begun that night. "For the Son of Man came to seek and to save what was lost" (Lk 19:10), and in His great love and mercy Jesus had come seeking me, as He does all His little lambs, and He had rescued me out of my lostness. It was His Holy Spirit who had led me to that little rural church and to Esther. And for all that time, her love and her prayers had been creating a spiritual hunger within me, preparing my heart to believe. Esther loved me to Jesus. That night He took me into His arms and I became forever His. I was home at last. Don Potter sings of it in this song that he wrote:

> *I'm a prisoner*
> *I can't explain this mystery.*
> *I'm a prisoner*
> *I don't want to be free.*
> *I'm a prisoner*
> *I'm just as caught as I ever was.*
> *I'm a prisoner of love.* [3]

Step All the Way Up to the Line, Please

In Rev 17:14 we read of a time when ten kings "...will make war against the Lamb, but the Lamb will overcome them because he is Lord of lords and King of kings – and with him will be his called, chosen, and faithful followers." Imagine that! His followers will be there with Him! These followers are described as called, chosen, and faithful... three levels of maturity that must all be progressively passed through. At each level there exists for each one of us the potential to disqualify ourselves.

First He calls us. To be called is to hear His voice. In the beginning that is the reason His voice comes to us – to extend to us the summons to follow Him. Our God is brilliantly creative and He is relentlessly personal with each one of us. Therefore we are called in many different ways. His voice can call through a song. It can overtake us unexpectedly in a time of great celebration and victory. It can come through a book, through an encounter with the wonder of creation, or in the devastating pain of personal tragedy and defeat. He can call through a dream. For me, He called through Esther. Rev 1:15 tells us that "His voice is like the sound of rushing waters." No other voice is like it. It calls to us, awakening our heart, creating within us an unsettling awareness that there is truly Someone bigger than ourselves... Someone we want desperately to rush home to.

I did not understand that Esther's love was God's voice calling to me. I did not know that all I had to do to be chosen was to hear and respond to the voice. We MUST hear. And we MUST respond. In Rev 1:12 John turned to see the voice that was speaking to him.

We must turn to see this One who speaks. His voice is life. His voice causes all things to rise up and live. Jn 5:28 says, "Do not be amazed at this, for a time is coming when all who are in their graves will hear his voice and come out…" Yes. Yes. His voice. His voice penetrates even death. Deep calling unto deep.

Oh, dearly beloved! He comes riding right up into our life – right face-to-face with us. His eyes of fire are ablaze with holy love. Do you see Him? Do you hear Him? He calls our name. Your name. He's calling your name. It's your time. It's your day. He's right in front of you. He's crying, "Will you ride with Me?" Everything within us is undone. We are consumed by His Presence. Our heart cries back, "Yes, Lord! Yes! With all that is in me, whatever the cost, I will ride with you!" The white horse rears. Its Rider throws His head to the wind and roars as a Lion, **"YOU! I CHOOSE YOU!"**

He chooses us. The word choose denotes the simple act of selecting something, the naming of something as the object desired. It implies the completion of a process of inspection, examination, and testing whereby we are proven. We are not chosen only once. He comes to us again and again, over and over, and calls, Will you ride with Me? He stands in our future and calls to us to come up higher. Then He watches to see if we want to be chosen. It is the very wanting of Him that qualifies us to be chosen.

At every place in the journey we are free to remain behind. He is the Sovereign Commander-in-Chief. He will not build His Kingdom from the ranks of those whose hearts are not aflame with passion. He chooses carefully. To those who love Him above all else, to those who hear the Voice and respond with desire, to those who refuse to be left behind, to them the promise is given. They are the called, chosen, and faithful followers who will ride with Him into battle.

I want that. I want to be there with Him. I want to always want Him. I want to never resist Him or hinder Him. I want to never turn away from His voice. I want to never disqualify myself. I want to soar on wings like eagles. I want to run and not grow weary. I want to walk and not be faint.

AND I WANT YOU TO BE THERE WITH ME, RIDING RIGHT
BESIDE ME, OUR ARMOR, OUR SHIELDS,
GLISTENING IN THE SUN.

DEARLY BELOVED, STEP ALL THE WAY UP TO THE LINE,
PLEASE.

CHAPTER THREE

The Valley of the Shadow of Death

We sat in a conference room around a large table. There were eight teachers, the school principal, and myself. As the meeting came to an end, the principal spoke with great concern. "Mrs. Johnson, unless something drastic should happen, both your sons will end up spending time in prison." They were twelve years old.

The Unfamiliar Descent

It was only months earlier, as the school year had just begun, that this principal had sought me out at the Open House for Parents. His words that night were like honey to a mother's heart, and when I went home I wrote them in my journal. "So you are Kevin and Danny's mother. What a pleasure it is to meet you. I am so delighted to have your boys with us. I have never seen two students who carried a greater potential for leadership. Why, if your boys announced they were selling tickets to the moon, every student in this school would be in line tomorrow to buy one!"

How quickly the honey had turned bitter. And the trip to the moon had been cancelled. It was difficult seeing through the tears as I drove home from the late afternoon conference. Storm clouds gathered in my heart and out loud I began to sing the song that was destined to carry me for many years to come.

Thou, O Lord,
Art a shield about me;
You're my glory
and the lifter up of my head.

For Thou , O Lord,
Art a shield about me;
You're my glory
and the lifter up of my head.

—Psalm 3: 3

That seventh-grade year Kevin and Danny accumulated more than two hundred detentions. Each detention was accompanied by a personal phone-call from the school office and a notice sent home to be signed. Together they were suspended fifty-two days. Their report cards came home with straight F's. In the early spring both of them were expelled and they failed the school year. The following year, convinced that all would be well, I home-schooled them. Then, our hopes high, we enrolled them in an all-boy's school. But in only a few short months they were expelled.

Our girls were attending a private Christian school at that time and we were very involved there. The men serving on the board of regents were our friends. But they were unable to accept our boys for enrollment. We found a smaller Christian school that was willing to take them. It was forty-five minutes from our home, and for several months I made the round-trip twice a day, taking them in the morning and picking them up in the afternoon, driving 3 hours a day to keep them in school. After four months they were again expelled.

They began smoking and were beginning to have incidences with alcohol. For many years they had been excellent athletes. In their younger years Hollis had always co-coached their teams and their games had been a bright and happy part of our life. But now they began being dismissed from their athletic teams. They were dismissed from youth group and from Sunday School and were no longer permitted to come.

In the midst of this time Hollis was promoted to a new position and we relocated to a new city and a new school district. It seemed like a ray of hope and a new beginning, as we had literally run out of schools. But it was only a very short time until they were expelled once more and were at home with no school to go to.

Our life began to unravel at an alarmingly rapid pace. Neither of them could hold down a job and were fired repeatedly. They were fifteen now and would often be gone from home for days at a time. Every night we would bolt and lock our car down to keep them from taking it. They began to become involved with crime and with the legal system and for years there were police cars in our driveway.

My life became consumed with driving them to jobs, often far away, often the night factory hours, to court hearings, to meetings with probation officers, to work-crew restitution, and to AA meetings. There was an endless parade of mandatory, court-ordered meetings that we had to attend as parents. For a long time I was naïve about their drug usage and the seriousness of their growing addiction. They became increasingly angry and violent. There was constant lying, and insidious, demonic laughter. There was disrespect, mockery, belligerence, and cursing... broken furniture, blood, and holes in the walls. There were threatening and harassing phone calls from dealers at all hours of the night. For years we slept with our wallets. They forged large checks that would cause our account to bounce. They sold their clothing and many precious gifts that we had given them in order to pay for drugs.

The storm did not last for just a season nor was it only for a time. It did not end and it did not get better. It only continued to grow darker and darker. We wanted to make it stop but nothing we did brought any change. My parents disowned me and would no longer come to our home. Many whom we loved wrote hateful, condemnatory letters to us telling us that we had failed as parents and were fully to blame. I can remember once coming home, pulling our car into the garage, and starting into the house. Suddenly I collapsed onto the cement garage floor, laid my head on the cement step, and began to sob and sob. *Oh God,* I cried, *I can't go in. I can't do it anymore.* Our home had become a prison.

Danny's drug usage became alarming. His speech became slurred and he was no longer able to track, or follow conversation. Both he and Kevin were admitted into the local hospital for several weeks but began using again as soon as they were discharged. I became panicky and would often cling to Hollis to make it through the night. I was unstable and felt desperate.

I called Danny's after-care drug counselor and asked to bring him in. I sat in the waiting area of the hospital while they met. After a long while the door opened and Danny came out first. He was swaggering and laughing and his eyes seemed hollow and far away as he came toward me. "Oh Mom," he said, "I'm gonna be dead before I'm twenty one. Just like Jimmy Morrison, Mom." I jumped out of my chair. I ran to Danny, took him in my arms, and called out at the top of my voice, "No! No! It's a lie from hell! You will live! And you will serve God!" I held onto him and kissed and kissed his neck. "I love you, Danny. I love you." He was sixteen and more than six feet tall. He took hold of me and his tears ran down my neck, wetting my shirt, as he pleaded desperately, "Please help me, Mom. Please help me. I'm so sick."

The week following Christmas we admitted Danny to a long-term treatment facility located three hours from our home. He would live there for the next several months. During his stay we made the trip twice a week for family group therapy, and again every Sunday for visiting. In time, Kevin was asked not to come as he was smuggling in drugs and cigarettes to Danny. It was an emotionally exhausting seven months during which we put almost twenty-five thousand miles on our car. Our hearts were filled with hope when at long last we packed up his things and brought him home. We celebrated and released a carload of helium balloons. On the first weekend back Danny began using again.

There were too many felonies to keep count. There were police officers in my yard, my kitchen, my basement and bedrooms. There were sirens, guns, search warrants, handcuffs, shackles, electronic beepers, and courtroom after courtroom. The judge said they ought to name a wing after us. We visited them in thirteen separate prisons, often leaving home in the early morning darkness to arrive in time for visitation. To this day I loathe the smell of microwave popcorn.

Death

Is there a moment when daylight ends and night begins? Or do the rays of light go out one by one until the spirit of man is broken? My life had grown very dark. A darkness so thick I could feel it. A darkness so cold that I was frightened. Years and years and years. Can the night last too long? Sobbing. Shaking. Screaming. Pounding the walls until my arms were black and blue. Thrashing through the night. Afraid. Always so afraid. Deep darkness. Desperation. Fear and torment. I wrote in my journal:

> *For you, O God, tested us;*
> *you refined us like silver.*
> *You brought us into prison*
> *and laid burdens on our backs.*
> *You let men ride over our heads;*
> *we went through fire and water,*
> *but you brought us to a place of abundance.*
> —Psalm 66:10-12

My soul was famished for the place of abundance. O Lord, my God, how long? How long?

Winter ended, summer came, and soon they would come home from prison. They were eighteen years old now and in my heart I still dreamed of high-school graduation. One night very late, while Hollis slept, I got up out of bed, put on shorts and t-shirt, and drove to the high-school baseball field. I parked the car and walked out onto the field.

The moon was shining full as I slowly walked the bases. Then I walked them a second time and stopped and stood at home plate. I could see them as clearly as though it were yesterday. My precious little boys. Running. Laughing. Their beautiful golden hair. Their uniforms of red and white. White and brown. I could see them older, their arms lean, tan, and muscular, poised as they stood waiting for the pitch. I heard the crack of the bat and saw them running like the wind. "I never saw any boys faster," they all said. I remembered all the times I had come up out of the bleachers erupting into shouts of joy as they slid into home.

Years of emotions erupted. This time I ran the bases. Then slowly, blinded with tears, I walked out and stood on the pitcher's mound. I remembered the game when Danny had struck out eighteen batters in a row. My heart broke and I cried out to heaven, "O Lord, please! Please! Let them play baseball again. Let the sun shine again, Lord!" Then I fell on the mound and wept and wept and wept.

That week I was admitted to the hospital and diagnosed with Crohn's disease. I spent three weeks in bed and lost twenty-eight pounds. I was not able to make the trip with Hollis to pick Kevin and Danny up, but they were home only a few days when *I knew*. I knew they would not be returning to school. And I knew there would be no more baseball games. Days after, in my journal, I recorded these words:

> *I was not sure what all God had purposed in this, but I found myself left with no life, very tired, eventually believing that my work was done, and finally a strong desire to go home. The ongoing burden of life left me numb. Things were so hard. I just wanted peace. I felt great love toward the Lord because I know He would not do anything toward me except out of His love to perfect me. I just felt very tired, and so aware that life is only pain, followed by more pain. Whereas I had once desired to be conformed to His image, now I just wanted release. There was no reward*

*for any of our labor. I began to long deeply to go home. I saw
the Father on a porch, sitting in a rocker. I wanted Him to
hold me on His lap, and rock me and rock me, and whisper
in my ear, "You did good, Patty. You did good." I began to
pray that He would take me. The second night I fell asleep
praying that. In the middle of the night I woke up from a
sound sleep and felt His Presence in the room. I sat upright
in my bed, and heard Him speak these words, "See, this day
I set before you life and death; therefore, choose life, Patty,
that you and your children may live."*

Ps 18:4-5,16-17 says:
*"The cords of death entangled me; the torrents of destruction
overwhelmed me. The cords of the grave coiled around me;
the snares of death confronted me. He reached down from
on high and took hold of me; he drew me out of deep waters.
He rescued me from my powerful enemy, from my foes, who
were too strong for me."*

Death. Destruction. The grave. Cords and torrents and snares.
Entangled and overwhelmed. But that night Jesus reached down, took
hold of me, and rescued me. He breathed His resurrection life and
power into me and raised me up from the dead. And even as the storm
raged on, there grew within the inner sanctuary of my heart a place of
refuge and fortification where fear could not penetrate.

The Potter's Hand

Kevin and Danny continued to be tossed to and fro. In a few
months we made them move out because of their violent tempers,
the drugs, and the disrespect. Their lives were chaotic and without
direction. Danny was soon incarcerated again. The following summer
we rented a cabin up north and Kevin came. He brought a young girl
with him whom we had never met. One bright afternoon, with dinner
still a long way off, I grabbed a book and curled up on the sofa that

faced out over the lake. I had been reading a long time when the cabin door opened and I looked up to see Angie. As she came through the door, the rays of the late afternoon sun caught her silhouette from behind and I realized that she was pregnant. I knew that she was carrying our first grandchild. Only a few weeks later we received a letter from Danny. Sitting on our sofa back home, I read the words he had written: I guess you know Jessica is pregnant with my baby.

Jessica pregnant...Angie pregnant...Two babies on the way. Jessica and Angie had been best friends since kindergarten. I had only been with them a few times and had never met any of their parents. They would be entering ninth grade in the fall and both babies were due in only three months.

Although my little granddaughters had not yet been born, I thought of them constantly. I thought of them all through the day and I thought of them all through the night. I felt conflict and turmoil in my heart. I had not known how tenaciously I was still holding on to my own dreams for Kevin and Danny. The foundation beneath my feet was cracking. Deeply entrenched roots within my battered heart were gasping for air. I could not build my own kingdom. I had to let go.

For years I had traveled, early every Monday morning, out the long country road to my friend's beautiful farm property. Week after week, year after year, we had sat at her kitchen table worshipping and praying to the Lord. We laughed, we cried, we shouted, we danced, we loved. That morning as I sat there with her again, I knew what I had to do. My heart felt stretched and the hill seemed too steep. A force as strong as iron resisted me. I screamed out in agony as the dream inside me contested its death. And then, with Mary's love making a way, I bowed my head and prayed through my tears: "Lord Jesus, I receive the babies. Lord, I thank you for sending them into our lives. Lord Jesus, I receive these little angels and all that they have for us." The dam broke and His peace flooded my heart.

Emily and Mandy were born six weeks apart. They stole their way into our hearts and we helped in every way we could. Their daddies drifted in and out and their relationships with Angie and Jessica became very turbulent.

One summer evening we were keeping Mandy for the night. She was just a little toddler. She loved her daddy and her eyes lit up that night when he unexpectedly came by. For a short time they played together. But then, with no good-byes, Danny went out through the garage and was off and gone to his own world.

Mandy wandered through every room looking for him. Her little legs climbed the stairs one at a time, searching every room upstairs for him, calling his name. I could not stop her. Finally, abandoned and rejected, her little heart burst, her lips quivered, and through broken sobs the words tumbled out. "Wh... wh... where Daddy g... g... go? Wh... wh... where Daddy g... g... go, Grandma?" My own tears burst forth as the stinking, rotten, pain and anguish of it all washed over me. I collapsed onto the floor, drawing Mandy into my lap, longing to shield her yet knowing I never could. Back and forth, back and forth we rocked, as I joined the wail of heaven.

They were part of our life for many years. We chased rainbows together, caught lightening bugs, built sand castles, and filled photograph albums. We ate ice-cream together at the county fair and blew out birthday candles with each other. As time passed, the families felt it best to sever ties with us. And as quickly as they had come into our lives, just as quickly they were gone.

I do not believe that I understood during that time the deep work that the Lord was doing in my heart. There were profound, profound changes taking place within me. I would never be the same. In that same season our youngest daughter, a single mom, moved home from Colorado with her little newborn son. He was only days older than Melissa's newest baby. My life and home were filled with babies and deep wells of love were being uncapped within me. The old familiar landscape of my heart was fading away and tiny new seedlings were being quietly planted by the Gardener. It would be years before they matured, but I could feel the faint stirrings of new life. To those grandchildren who were there and who were part of it, the deposit you left in me will bear fruit forever.

So many times during those years, Jesus and I would just sit together quietly, just being with each other, as I struggled to embrace the new place, and to even lay aside personal dreams for my own life. In those times I would sing to Him out of my overwhelming love for all that He was to me. He would give me words to heal the loneliness. This is one of those songs.

Your steadfast love, is like a river
Your steadfast love, it washes me
When the road seems long,
and there are no answers,
Your steadfast love, it anchors me.

And when the night is all around me,
The wind blows strong
And I can't go on,
Jesus, your hand, it reaches for me
And your steadfast love,
It anchors me.

CAN YOU SEE THAT PORCH LIGHT
SHINING STRAIGHT AHEAD?
RIGHT THERE.
STRAIGHT AHEAD.
DO YOU SEE IT?
FATHER IS SITTING OUT TONIGHT ON HIS ROCKER.
GO ON.
RUN, BELOVED. RUN.
CRAWL UP ON HIS LAP.
LET HIM HOLD YOU CLOSE.
HE'S EXPECTING YOU.
THERE'S SOMETHING HE WANTS TO WHISPER IN YOUR EAR.

CHAPTER FOUR

Dungeons and Dragons

When the king of Moab saw *"...that the battle had gone against him, he took with him seven hundred swordsmen to break through to the king of Edom, but they failed. Then he took his firstborn son, who was to succeed him as king, and offered him as a sacrifice on the city wall. The fury against Israel was great; they withdrew and returned to their own land"* (2Kgs 3:27).

"But woe to the earth and the sea, because the devil has gonedown to you! He is filled with fury, because he knows that his time is short" (Rev 12:12).

The Destroyer

Every life is precious to God. When conception occurs within the womb, God breathes into that tiny form the breath of life and blesses and ordains it to be an irreplaceable part of His divine plan. He is fervently in love with each of us and sets His heart upon our future, longing that we should run like horses and soar like eagles. His love is unbounded and without limit. He watches jealously over us, and warns all in Mt 18:10, "See that you do not look down on one of these little ones. For I tell you that their angels in heaven always see the face of my Father in heaven." How is it then that for some His plan is seemingly aborted? How is it that multitudes,

multitudes of lives, end up imprisoned in shadowy wastelands, held captive in dungeons of darkness, the very fabric of their souls torn, marred, and violated?

Dr. Gregory Reid is an ordained minister and the author of eleven books. *Nobody's Angel* is the raw and brutal story of his life; a journey into the horrors of the Dark Side. Obsessed with the occult, victimized by pedophiles, and on his way to becoming an adept occultist, Gregory surrendered his life to Jesus at age fifteen. *Nobody's Angel* is the account of his decades-long search for answers to his tormented childhood. In the opening of his book, he writes:

> *Only those who have been almost irreparably traumatized can fully understand such loss, frustration and overwhelming sadness. I'm not like you. I'm a patchwork child, who with trembling hands has had to reconstruct a fragmented mess without a sense of time, or age, or a map of maturity, or the glue of consistency… And [this book] is for little Gregory, the child who was the heir-apparent to an evil he didn't want, almost received, and now is forever free from. It's for the child in the pictures without a soul who could only look forward to Satan's destiny and a short life spilled out into eternal Nothing.* [4]

A patchwork child… without a soul… Stephen Hill is a passionate missionary evangelist who was used mightily by God in the late nineties, during the Brownsville Revival in Pensacola, Florida. His fiery preaching brought hundreds to the altar. Stephen has written a book, *Time to Weep*, in which he shares an unusually graphic and riveting dream that the Lord gave him concerning the destructive nature of the enemy. Following is the description of Satan as portrayed in his dream.

> *…suddenly the door swung open. There, standing in the doorway, was a huge, towering man, over seven feet tall. He*

stepped inside and stood like a statue at the entrance.

No one noticed.

Looking into his eyes was like staring face-to-face into death. He looked straight at me but didn't flinch. I knew at that moment I was only in the room as a witness, unable to do anything. He looked at me fiercely, streetwise. From his hardened face came a frozen stare that will remain forever imprinted on my mind. He was angry.

He stood motionless. His fiery eyes roamed the room as if he were seeking out a familiar face – someone to burn. Then the horror began. He raised his left foot into the air and slammed it to the ground. The floor shook. Nobody moved. I stood in shock as the employees took no notice.

Then he raised his right foot, slammed it to the ground and again shook the floor…

In this man's left hand was a paper sack. Reaching in, he pulled out a bottle of whiskey. He raised the vial over his head and soaked his face. Within seconds his entire head was covered in the liquor. It filled his mouth and overflowed, pouring down his chin. His forehead was doused, obviously blurring his vision, as the burning alcohol flowed over his eyes.

With the bottle drained, he began shaking his head violently back and forth, his long stringy hair soaked in venom, whipping the air, slinging the whiskey everywhere. Nobody noticed; nobody moved.

Then he reached into his left pocket and pulled out a large, silver butcher knife. The blade glistened as he raised it over his head. With his eyes still roaming the room he let out a scream that pierced the air. The deadening cry shook the building. Finally he got the people's attention.[5]

"He let out a scream that pierced the air..." We are living in a day in which the enemy has released his war cry. In the opening passage of this chapter from Rev 12:12, we read that the devil has come down to us, filled with fury, because he knows that his time is short. *Fury*, translated *megas thymos*, means great violent movement, impetuous motion or passion of the mind, powerful inward feelings of fierce rage, and frenzy. In the preceding passage from 2Kgs 3:27 we read about this same fury. The king of Moab, unable to prevail in battle, petitioned the powers of darkness to his aid by offering up his son as a blood sacrifice on the city wall. This incited Satan to release his fury against the opposing army, Moab's enemy, which was Israel. Satan's fury enfeebled and paralyzed Israel's army and prohibited their advancement. Scripture records that they withdrew and returned to their own land.

Satan is called the "ruler of the kingdom of the air." Jesus calls him the "prince of this world." As a ruler over a kingdom, he has a throne and he exercises power. He is a created being. He was created in perfection, wisdom, and beauty, and was blameless in his ways. But his heart became proud. Wickedness was found in him and he was filled with violence and corruption. Showing contempt for that which is holy, he set his heart to make himself like the Most High, and was driven in disgrace from the mount of God. He opposes man with rage and hostility because man is created in God's image and is the object of His redeeming love. He comes to steal and kill and destroy our lives. [6]

Plundered

There is a beautiful passage of scripture in Isa 54:1 that speaks of the *desolate woman*. The word desolate means to be stunned, devastated, destroyed; to be astonished, appalled; to be solitary. It denotes something so horrible that it can leave a person outside the reach of others. It is used in 2 Sam 13:20 to describe Tamar after her brother Amnon raped her. "And Tamar lived in her brother Absalom's house, a desolate woman."

The same passage from Isaiah speaks in verse four of this desolate woman *suffering shame*. The word for suffering shame, *bos*, means to be confounded, disappointed, disgraced, kept waiting, deceived. It often occurs in contexts of humiliation, public disgrace, and shattered human emotions. *Bos* denotes confusion, embarrassment, or dismay when things do not turn out as expected. Sometimes there is a strong connotation of guilt or disillusionment and a broken spirit.

These words furnish a piercing description of the enemy's work. It is a description too well known to those who have experienced it. In 2Cor. 12:7 the apostle Paul uses another strong word that unmasks the enemy's nature. "…there was given me a thorn in my flesh, a messenger of Satan, to torment me." This word for torment means to strike with the fists, to beat, to be brutally treated. It comes from a root word that means punishment. Its victims suffer unmerciful mental anguish, their minds being twisted and thrown into a state of frantic whirling. It is the spirit behind self-abuse and self-inflicted pain. It is the spirit behind violent thrashing and tormented screaming.

In his book, *Our Hands Are Stained With Blood*, Michael L. Brown, a professor of Hebrew Bible and Jewish Studies, speaks of the brutal honesty that characterizes the relationship between a Jew and his God. He illustrates by sharing just a few lines from a prayer by a Jew named Zvi Kolitz. The prayer, written against the flaming backdrop of the Holocaust, is the fiery cry of a heart tormented and strained to the utmost.

> *…I believe in You, God of Israel, even though You have done everything to stop me from believing in You. I believe in Your laws even if I cannot excuse Your actions…*
>
> *I want to say to You that now, more than in any previous period of our eternal path of agony, we, we the tortured, the humiliated, the buried alive, the burned alive, we the insulted, the mocked, the lonely, the forsaken by God and man – we have the right to know what are the limits of Your forbearance?*
>
> *I should like to say something more: Do not put the rope under too much strain, lest, alas, it snap! The test to which You have put us is so severe, so unbearably severe, that You should*

– You must – forgive those members of Your people who, in their misery, have turned from You…

You have done everything to make me stop believing in You. Now lest it seem to You that You will succeed by these tribulations to drive me from the right path, I notify You, my God and God of my father, that it will not avail You in the least! You may insult me, You may castigate me, You may take from me all that I cherish and hold dear in the world, You may torture me to death – I shall believe in You, I shall love You no matter what You do to test me!

And these are my last words to You, my wrathful God: nothing will avail You in the least. You have done everything to make me renounce You, to make me lose faith in You, but I die exactly as I have lived, a believer! [7]

Even the corporate shared soul of a nation or people group can be sabotaged through the hand of those who hate them. Atrocities that defy reasoning bear down upon man, threatening to irreparably extinguish his spirit, darkening his eyes and rendering him unable to discern between the kingdom of light and the kingdom of darkness. In Mt. 12:20, 21 God says of His Son: "A bruised reed he will not break, and a smoldering wick he will not snuff out, til he leads justice to victory. In his name the nations will put their hope." The Carpenter of Nazareth always heals and restores and always causes justice to be victorious. Out of the heart that puts its hope in Him will come the piercing cry of Zvi Kolitz, I shall believe in You, I shall love You no matter what You do to test me!

Heaven's Healing Balm

I will break down gates of
bronze and cut through bars of iron.
I will give you the treasures of
darkness, riches stored in secret places…

—Isaiah 45:2, 3

Shrouded in fog, encased behind rigid, twisted bars of iron, there looms a place of darkness where men, women, and children have been taken captive and are being held prisoners by ancient lords of revenge and retribution. Jesus, that great Shepherd of the sheep, comes to seek and to save these special ones who are His *treasures*, kingdom riches stored in secret places. He breaks down the gates of bronze and cuts through the bars of iron. He lifts each one from the dungeon (Isa 42:7) and says to the captives, "Come out," and to those in darkness, "Be free!" (Isa 49:9).

The beloved apostle John speaks in his epistle of these tormented ones. He reveals the only healing balm that is powerful enough to shatter the iron bars of fear and bring release. In 1Jn 4:18 he writes, *"There is no fear in love. But perfect love drives out fear, because fear has to do with punishment. The one who fears is not made perfect in love."* In this passage, the word that John uses for punishment is the word that Paul uses for the torment of the enemy in 2Cor. 12:7. John is declaring that fear is the result of the enemy tormenting us, striking and beating us, and twisting our minds. This torment of the enemy is driven out through our love. Even as the Most High drove Satan in disgrace from the mount of God, so shall the perfection of love drive Satan's torment from our hearts.

Perfected love is costly. Like a highly-prized vintage wine, perfected love requires time and processing under rigorous conditions in order to reach maturity. Fully ripened love always bears the fragrance of the One whose name is Love. This perfected love is lavish, excessive, daring and reckless. It is bold and confident and shines brightly. It is impossible to contain and delights in wastefulness. It does not live by rules and cannot be offended. Such is the love that overcomes fear.

A Horn of Salvation

So very quietly Jesus enters our darkness. Through our tears we behold His form. He lowers His head as He maneuvers the shallow stairway leading down into our dank and musty dungeon. We have lost count of the times He has come and the hours He has spent here with us in this place. When all our strength was gone and we despaired to go another step, always He came to silence the scream in our heart. Again and again and again, His arms gathered us close, as he comforted and reassured us, bathing our wounds and our brokenness in the tenderness of His love.

But this night is not the same. He does not come and sit as in times past. He is not here to stay. He stands, looking down at us, and His eyes seem almost as fire. He does not wear the simple, sturdy garment of the Shepherd – the one we have so loved to nestle up against, rich with the earthen scent of the fields and the night air. No. Not tonight. This night the strong hues of purple and crimson catch our breath away as they play upon His robe in hints of royalty. This night our eyes fasten upon the glint of His sword and our heart begins to pound. Why is He here? What is different? Has He come to slay the great dragon?

Now for the first time He speaks and there is great finality in His voice. "We shall not be meeting here again," He says. "The time has come for you to leave this place."

Leave? Fear grips our heart like a vise. *Oh, no! No! No! Never could we find our way out of this dungeon!* Has He forgotten how bruised and torn we are? Why can't He come and sit and stay? Hot, scalding tears well up within us. He is being unreasonable.

But He has already turned to go. *"My little one, I have come to lead you out of this place. I have come to teach you. I have come to break open a whole new dimension of love within you. You do not yet know My love, but I am going to cause you to become rooted and established in My perfect love. You shall see the iron bars shatter and you will become free. You will laugh at fear. Come, quickly! Lean into Me and trust Me."*

I SHALL MAKE YOU THE DRAGON-SLAYER.

Praise be to the Lord, the God of Israel,
because he has come and has redeemed his people.
He has raised up a horn of salvation for us ...
salvation from our enemies
and from the hand of all who hate us---
to rescue us from the hand of our enemies,
and to enable us to serve him without fear...
to give his people the knowledge of salvation
through the forgiveness of their sins,
because of the tender mercy of our God,
by which the rising sun will
come to us from heaven
to shine on those living in darkness
and in the shadow of death,
to guide our feet into the path of peace.

—Luke 1:68-79

CHAPTER FIVE

Though I Have Fallen, I Will Rise
—Micah 7:8

Chatter began to fill the room as most everyone had finished their personality test and had now begun sharing their results with one another. I tried to calm the swirl of panic rising inside of me. It was a simple test with only twenty questions. "For each question choose the answer that most consistently describes your personality." But I was barely through the first few questions as my eye ran anxiously down the page hoping to find just one that I would know how to answer.

When the workshop ended, our little group headed for the ice-cream parlor. We sat around the table as everyone laughed and shared. I felt shut out. Finally someone asked, "Well, Patty, you're being really quiet. How'd your test go?" Anger erupted like a volcano. "I don't HAVE a personality!" I snapped. "I'm ALL of the answers, ALL of the time. I'm just whatever people tell me to be. I don't HAVE a personality!"

PART 1

The Entrance of Truth

I was 45 years old and I wanted off the treadmill and out of the cage. In my heart I knew I was running as hard as I could at life, and yet I never seemed to get beyond the confines of some mysterious, ignominious cage that held me prisoner. All around me I felt walls trapping me… pushing against me and pushing against me and pushing against me. My heart ached to scale the walls and live outside the cage.

There began to form within me a frustration and an agitation. I watched as other women, some even younger than me, were doing things that I knew were the very things that I had been created to do. I could feel the sound of dreams beginning to rumble somewhere deep inside of me, as if they too were groaning to be set free. At first the sound was only a faint ripple that could barely be trusted. But the rumble grew more and more insistent and disruptive, abrasively intruding into my fear and deception. In time I became brave enough to test the waters. A stubborn spark of faith pushed its tiny hand out from my pitiful ash heap of defeat and ignited the dreams. As if in response to my faith, far out on the distant horizon there began to come into focus a place that was calling my name.

It was a beautiful autumn. It was October 1994 and I had traveled to Charlotte, North Carolina, to attend a conference there. For the past several years I had been reading the books and the writings of several men and women who would be speakers at this gathering. Through their books I had come to know and trust these people. There was a hurt inside me so big that I could not separate myself from it and I went to North Carolina with a hunger and desperation to hear God's voice.

The conference crowd was large and the schedule moved quickly. As so often happened, I felt lonely and out of place. Strong emotions were swirling inside me as once again I wrestled with the hopelessness that there were no answers for me. The last day of the conference came and the lunch crowds were returning and gathering outside the building as they waited for the doors to open. I could not quiet my heart.

I needed to be alone and went and stood under a large shade tree in the midst of the crowd. In a show of impatience I stomped my foot. "Lord Jesus," I said, "this is Patty. From Ohio. Lord, I drove all the way down here because I need to hear a word from You. Lord, my heart has been ripped apart and I don't know how to go on. Lord, I'm asking you to speak to me. I don't care how hard a word it is or even if you have to discipline me. I just want to hear Your voice."

I went into the auditorium and took an aisle seat halfway down as the musicians were beginning to play. As we entered worship I could strongly sense the presence of the Lord behind me. I turned and in my spirit I could see Him far at the back of the room. I could see Him begin to come forward, striding down the aisle with great purpose and appointment, His gaze fixed straight ahead. He was dressed in a tunic of royalty, majestic and kingly. His demeanor was that of a warrior, the Mighty Man of War come to triumph over his enemies. (Isa42:13) When He reached the place where I was standing, He stopped beside me and turned to face me. "I'm moving on, Patty. And if you choose to stay here and nurse your wounds, I'll be gone. It's time to get down off my lap." And then He quickly moved on.

His words jolted me. Arrested me. He was offering me an ultimatum. And He had made the ultimatum very clear. His lap was what I longed for and where I wanted to be. Yet He was asking me to follow Him into an unknown future. He was indeed moving on and it was my choice if I would be with him. Down off His lap … into my future … I could not fathom it.

Quietly my heart whispered yes to Him.

As the gathering drew to a close, an invitation was given for anyone to come forward who had not been personally ministered to. The line was long, the evening was late, and I had a lengthy trip ahead of me in the morning. But none of it mattered. I had come to hear from God.

When the conference leader began to pray for me, she said,

"The Lord is showing me that your inner man is in great turmoil. You are hungry and starved for the word of God. The Lord wants to feed you with His word." I did not understand, and so I shared with her that I spent many hours reading His word. "Oh, yes," she replied, "the Lord shows me that you are receiving great knowledge of his Word in your mind, but it is not reaching your spirit man. It's as if you can't receive good news."

The following evening I pulled the car into our garage and carried my suitcase up the stairs to our bedroom. I was home. Home to the same rooms that I had filled with my tears. Home to the same familiar turmoil waiting to swallow me again. But I knew that I stood at a divine juncture.

The Lord had seen that young woman standing under the tree. He had seen her stomp her foot and had heard her desperate cry. And He had answered from heaven. Etched in my heart was the picture of Jesus as He had moved away from me and headed on. (Lk 4:42-44) My majestic King! Gloriously mighty in battle! He wanted me with Him. Of that I was certain. And I was also certain of this: that my spirit man was about to receive a long overdue banquet of good news as I faced into the future and ran hard after Him.

It was hard giving the Lord permission to not explain everything. For years I had always thought that there would be a day when the Lord would come to me. I thought that He was waiting for it as eagerly as I was. We would sit together in some stately wood-paneled room over fresh glasses of cold iced tea, and He would speak tenderly to me concerning the past years. He would want me to understand. He would answer all my *"whys."* He would justify the heartache and make everything alright. Slowly I realized that was not going to happen. He did not hold Himself accountable to me. He had simply extended to me the invitation to climb down off His lap and follow Him into my future.

It can be quite unraveling when our perceptions and expectations of the Lord are challenged. When He does not do what we thought He would do, or what we feel He should do, we are left humbled by His sovereignty. For some, it can be so offensive that it causes them to stumble. (Lk 7:23) For those who are teachable, it produces a cutting away of the self-life, a pruning in the inner man which makes way for childlike trust to find lodging in our heart.

As I sought to trust the Lord and make the clean cut from the past, there came a day when He brought to my remembrance my dream of the house. I remembered the upstairs room and the magical closet full of gowns. I remembered that the room had represented my future and that suddenly, in the dream, the old me had appeared there. I had not thought of it in years. She certainly hadn't knocked! Nor did it seem that anyone had let her in. Yet there she was! All of a sudden I understood that she was there because everywhere I went I took her with me! I grabbed my old journal from the shelf and turned quickly to the pages where I had recorded the dream. Now, seeing with fresh revelation, it all became so clear.

In my journal I had written that although I thought this woman had come to take the gowns, instead she had just quietly sat down on a large bed that appeared in the room. I also recorded that as she sat on the bed she was partially exposed. In dream language, this bed represented my private, most intimate thoughts, even my spiritual and emotional needs. The bed was large because the old me occupied a large amount of my thoughts. She was enthroned atop the baggage that I carried. She was always present and I could not separate myself from her. I walked in her shadow… a shadow that came from a very deep sense of shame. (Rev 3:18)

It was as if the Lord had pulled out the first of the gowns from the closet… the small one… and that I was about to step into it. That day I made peace with the years that had gone before. I forgave the past for all the ways that it had disappointed me and fallen short of my dreams. I chose to bestow honor, dignity and respect upon it and I declared that in the annals of eternity it would be weighed in the scales of justice and found not wanting, in that my God would cause it to work together with all things for my good and for His purpose in my life. I spoke a redemptive blessing upon it, thanking God that He was with me through it all, and I forgave myself for taking on the garment of shame. Even as Shem and Japheth for their father Noah (Gen 9:23), I took the garment of praise, laid it across my shoulders, then walked in backwards and covered the nakedness of my past. I resolved that it would no longer overshadow me and that I would no longer identify myself as a victim imprisoned in a cage of hurt.

Spiritually, I felt as though I had been instantly fast forwarded light-years ahead. It was like being shot out of a cannon into an unfamiliar place of cleanness and brightness where self-condemnation did not exist. I could feel His song of love over my life and heaven smiling down upon me. It was a new place of wholeness and hope, a place from which I could now welcome Him as Teacher.

The Lord is quite different in His role as Teacher than in His role as Dresser of our wounds. As Teacher He comes to build within our hearts the highways to Zion. As Teacher He comes to grow us up into Him, desiring ardently that in every aspect we should become like Him. As Teacher He enlists us for duty, fitting us for battle, equipping us as warriors, and transforming us into bold, zealous, and fiery dragon-slayers.

My introduction into this new facet of His nature came quickly. The battleground was one I knew well… a place where again and again the enemy had trumped me. It seemed to be a trio of three chummy bedfellows: anger, jealousy, and selfish ambition. I could not always clearly separate them. Nor could I make sense of their strangling hold upon me. Prayer had brought only measured victory.

Sometimes it felt like a large manhole with its cover removed. I would be innocently walking along and then, without warning, down, down I would go as the blackness swallowed me. I loathed it. I could not rid my heart of the impurity and it wore me out as I grieved before the Lord.

Finally there arose from out of my innermost being a strong cry to heaven for victory. Defeated, and wet with tears and perspiration, I stood in my bedroom one day declaring at the top of my lungs, "I won't go there anymore! I refuse to fall into that hole ever again!" I began to shout Mt 1:21: "You are to give him the name Jesus, because he will save his people from their sins." I shouted it over and over and over, pacing the floor with loud cries and tears to the one who could save me from death, (Heb 5:7).

> *"You are to give him the name Jesus, because he will save his people from their sins. You are to give him the name Jesus, because he will save his people from their sins. You are to give him the name Jesus, because he will save his people from their sins. Save me, O Lord, from this ugliness."*

My heart ached to be free from the uncleanness and I cast myself upon His redeeming mercy. I had nowhere to turn but to Him, "...the Lamb of God, who takes away the sin of the world!" (Jn 1:29).

That day its iron grip over me was broken. It retreated, burrowing itself deep in the cavernous recesses of my heart, from whence it emerged only rarely to whimper. Years later there awaited a season when, in the appointments of God, the rage would rise up one last time. God does business with us as we are able. When that time came, the Lord, having trained me well to handle the sword of love, would require me to strike the fatal deathblow.

> *All of them wearing the sword,*
> *all experienced in battle, each with his sword at his side,*
> *prepared for the terrors of the night.*   —*Song of Songs 3:8*

Who is this One who takes what is injured and heals it? Who is this One who takes what is broken and rebuilds it? Who is this Planter of dreams who answers to no one? He lifts the yoke from our neck and bends down to feed us. He rides upon the cherubim and soars on the wings of the wind. In majesty He rides forth victoriously in behalf of truth, humility and righteousness. Who is this One who calls Himself the Resurrection and the Life?

> *Your righteousness reaches to the skies,*
> *O God, you who have done great things.*
> *Who, O God, is like you?*
> *Though you have made me see*
> *troubles, many and bitter, you will restore my life*
> *again; from the depths of the earth*
> *you will again bring me up.*
> *You will increase my honor and comfort me once again.*
> —*Psalm 71:19-21*

Jesus comes as the Healer of all those places within you that have been crushed and worn down by life. He lifts up your head. He restores your wounded heart to trust again. He stirs up vision within you afresh and anew and releases you to expect good things. He is the eternal Keeper of His vineyard, a vineyard whose grapes drip sweet wine. He is the Keeper of His plans for your life. The words below, spoken over me prophetically during my healing, bear testimony to His enduring love that reaches down and pulls us up into the brightness of a new tomorrow.

> *"Truly I have sent a refreshing your way. Not a refreshing, a resurrection. I have brought you forth. I've brought you forth from the dead, actually. And when you had given up ... and when you had given up and said, "I've just had it all. I've had enough," that's when I reached down and pulled you up and said, "Yes, there's life here. There's life here." And daughter, I've brought you into the resurrection life and the resurrection power. That's what I want you to grasp hold of. And I do not want defeat admitted ever again. I don't want you ever to*

even look and say, you know, that the grave would be more comfortable than where I am. But daughter I want you to look up, look up, for the days, the days are looking brighter. The star, the star, the morning star Jesus Christ, is shining brighter. It's getting brighter and your walk will get brighter. You have passed through the valley of the shadow of death, and you have come through that, and I want you to understand you're walking out of that, into the sunlight.

(From deep within my spirit there came a loud, strong cry of deliverance as I shouted, "Yeeeeeeeeeeeessss!")

Keep pursuing, saith the Lord. Yes, O yes! Amen! Yes amen! Hallelujah! Nothing is ahead like what was in the past. No torment like there … there was a severe torment in the past. There's none of that ahead.

PART 2

Who is This Coming up from the Wilderness?

The Lord had not forgotten the dreams that had begun to stir down deep inside of me. He knew that my future was hidden in those dreams and He was about to turn the rumble into a seismic roar. In the fall of 1999 I drove to Nashville, Tennessee, for a conference called Women on the Frontline. Everything in me longed passionately to be on the frontline for God's kingdom. Even so, I did not realize the significance of this conference for my life.

Once in the conference setting, I faced head-on the old familiar feelings of insignificance and condemnation. I had gained considerable ground over these lies and I was walking in a great measure of freedom. But I believe the demons, knowing this place was about to become their graveyard, rallied one last time. Pr 31:14 says of the noble woman: *"She is like the merchant ships, bringing her food from afar."* When we thirst for God, when our heart desires Him above all else, we will travel as far as needed to find the spiritual food that we crave. I had traveled a long way and God was about to infuse me with a jolt of spiritual voltage that would make shambles of my old paradigms.

I don't remember exactly when it happened. But at some point early on an older woman took the platform. She was introduced as Eileen Vincent. She was at once captivating and delightfully mischievous, and it was instantly apparent that the Holy Spirit adored her. She said that she had read about this conference at her home in Texas and that God had told her she was to come and speak. How outrageously and refreshingly audacious! And that was exactly why the Lord had brought her!

Eileen shared her amazing testimony of how God had unexpectedly lifted her out of the place that others had defined for her and had thrust her into His dreams for her life. She shared how for years she and her husband had traveled in many nations doing ministry in a time when it was considered quite improper for women to preach. The platform chairs were all reserved for men. "Women could share," she said, her eyes twinkling, "but not preach. And that, only if they had a hat on!"

With her fiery and passionate style, Eileen not only brought her message, she was her message. I drank that night not only from her words but from the bold impact of her life. With great conviction she shared the following story that God had given her to tell and which I relate in my own words with her permission.

One particular evening, as she and her husband were driving to a revival meeting, Eileen was aware in her spirit that her husband was feeling no anointing and had no thought or direction on what to preach. "You don't have the word, do you?" she inquired in her British accent.

"No," he replied.

There was a long silence.

"You have it, don't you?" he said.

"Yes," she lamented, home fresh from South Korea and still stirred by the overflow of all that God had done. "But what difference does it make? For I am not allowed to preach." But that night it made all the difference. When they arrived at the gathering, Alan had a chair placed on the platform for Eileen. And when it came time that night for the word to be released, he introduced Eileen in his place.

"I had my hat on," Eileen confessed, "but I didn't share Honey, I preached!"

In the days that followed, she was nearly overcome with condemnation for what she had done, convinced that she had disgraced her Lord and Savior. For days she wept, after which Jesus, the Lover of her soul, came and spoke to her. "Eileen, He said, the gifts that I have given to you do not belong to you. And Eileen, the gifts that I have given to you do not belong to the men. Eileen, the gifts that I have given to you belong to Me."

Tears welled in my eyes that night as the Holy Spirit hovered over the weary waters of my heart. The leather straps of man-made doctrines were coming unloosed. Wholeness and restoration were seeping into the fragmented shards of my personality as the Great Physician moved skillfully to redeem those things that had been lost… all that the years had stolen. Warm, healing rays of hope hung their pegs firmly in my heart. Eileen's testimony had unmercifully shattered the walls of my prison and fireworks exploded inside of me as the dreams that I had felt guilty for believing in now stood confidently erect and at attention. An unshakable sense of purpose and destiny began to take hold of me.

In my personal library are four books that have carried me in season and out of season. They are the biographies and sermons of Aimee Semple McPherson, Kathryn Johanna Kuhlman, Smith Wigglesworth, and Maria Woodworth-Etter. The picture on the cover of each book is the same. The beloved servant of God stands, one hand holding the opened Scripture, the other hand upraised to heaven as the Word is boldly preached. Although the pages of each book are marked and worn, and have been read many times, it has always been the covers that have arrested my heart. Time after time, when I felt I could not go on, I would go to my bookshelf, pull down the books, hold them tightly to my heart, and weep.

I had not understood in those times that deep was calling unto deep. I had not known that the same eternal streams of glory that flowed through those pictures were gurgling in my own heart. On the Sunday morning following the conference in Nashville, I went into church, sat down in our usual spot, and opened the bulletin. My eyes fastened upon the words *Preaching With Power* and my heart did a somersault! The class was being offered through a local Bible college. I filled out the enrollment form and wrote my check.

As I took a seat on the first night of class, I watched the room fill up with all young men. The weeks passed as I attended the classes, read the required textbooks and wrote the required assignments. The course neared its end and still I could not say the word 'preach' out loud in the same sentence with my own name. Whenever I would try, the word would stick in my throat and a feeling of unworthiness would settle on me.

On the final night of class, each student was given the opportunity to preach for five minutes. One of the young men asked if our grade would be affected if we went over the time. I had not thought about that. And I did not care. The yearning, the fervor, the ache to preach burned inside me. It was as if it had been shut up within me for a lifetime. Waiting… Just waiting… Oh! My God and King! It seemed as if I had been waiting for this night forever.

I was last. As I came to the podium, an overwhelming sense of joy and strong personal identity flooded me. Standing there speaking, I knew that God had called me to deliver His word into the earth. As one who had cherished and fed upon His word for over twenty years, I preached from the very wells of salvation deep within me. I felt the Lord's tangible pleasure with me all the way, as if He too had been waiting for this night. When I finished, one of the instructors stretched out his arm, pointed his finger at me, and declared, "Woman, God's called you to preach. And you can preach in my pulpit anytime you want."

In the months and years to come, God solidified my assurance of the call. It came in many ways. But mostly it came quietly in my times alone with Him. He tested my heart. He tested my strength. He tested my desire. He weaned me from the fear of man and made note of my quickness to obey His Voice. I remember the day and the place in our home when, knowing full well what He was asking, I presented myself before Him and invited Him to clothe me in the call. And the deal was sealed.

The following Sunday morning, as our church service ended, the sleek, light, transparent podium was moved in order to clear a space upfront for ministry. I watched as the ushers placed it off to the side of the sanctuary in a corner. I stood looking at it for a long time and my heart began to pound. Finally, amidst all the activity and noise, unnoticed by anyone, I approached the podium. It was a very private moment between the Holy Spirit and me. I placed my hands on it and began to softly cry. In my heart it represented all the places and all the people that God would send me to. He alone would open the doors. Quietly I spoke to the podium.

I HAVE AN APPOINTMENT WITH YOU.
AND I'LL BE THERE.

Lord, you have assigned me my portion and my cup;
you have made my lot secure.
The boundary lines have fallen for me in pleasant places;
surely I have a delightful inheritance.

—Psalm 16:5,6

CHAPTER SIX

Tonight I Have Asked You to Dance

She gathered her notes and approached the podium. I was sitting in the front row and as she picked up the microphone, she turned and spoke to me. "Ma'am, can I pray for you before I start?" She asked me to come and stand in front of her as she began to share the words that the Lord had stirred in her heart concerning my life.

And then she said, "The Lord tells me that it is in that place of praise and worship, of dancing before Him, where you just get undignified, He says there lies your victory over ALL things. That is what has kept you, and that is what's gonna continue to keep you, is that place where you can just get down and dirty with the Lord, so to speak."

Contending for Our Garment

In John 8:1-11 the story is recorded of an encounter between Jesus and a woman. The encounter takes place at dawn as Jesus appears in the temple courts. It is a significant setting. Dawn is the time when darkness gives way and transitions into light. Dawn is the emerging of a new day.

Crowds had gathered in the early morning light, and Jesus sat teaching them, when the teachers of the law and the Pharisees came bringing a woman. Saying they had caught her in the very act of adultery, they made her stand before the group. The man is blatantly missing, and we are only left to speculate if he was one of their own. They wanted her stoned.

Roused from her nighttime activities, rudely ordered to put something on, and forcibly compelled through the winding streets to the temple court, the woman now stood surrounded by the angry voices of accusation and condemnation… the voices of men… important men in long robes. Her heart was racing. Where was she? The morning air chilled her and she had no covering. What was happening?

Suddenly she watched as one at a time her accusers dropped their stones and began to go away, their own unrighteousness unmasked by the man who was sitting on the ground. They had called Him Jesus. She watched until only He was left and she was alone with Him.

As the morning light made its way above the horizon, and the distant memories of the night began to fade, she looked into the eyes of the only man who had the right to judge her. Never had she felt such compassion. He spoke. And deep, deep, down into the most forsaken corner of her heart, down into a lifetime of loneliness and abuse, His words tumbled, tumbled, tumbled… somersaulting, spilling upside down, electrifying her spirit: "Then neither do I condemn you. Go now and leave your life of sin."

How long had it been since she had run? But that morning she flew down the cobble streets as though the very wind of heaven were carrying her. She ran and she ran as the words of the Stranger bubbled up inside her. Oh Mama! Oh Papa! If only you could have met Him!

Do you suppose it might have been a Tuesday? Perhaps a Friday? Were there clients on her calendar that day? Were there men waiting for her when she arrived home? Was today the day that he was coming… the one she loved… the one who had been a friend to her? Perhaps she fell. Perhaps she fell twice. But the day came when she never fell again.

WHEN YOU MEET HER IN HEAVEN
WILL YOU WANT TO HEAR HER STORY AGAIN?
IS THIS YOUR STORY?

The transformation of a life from brokenness to wholeness is a profound occurrence. All the powers of hell stand ready to defeat us. It requires great resolution and courage to redefine our nature. It is a rending of the very fabric of our life. Paul says in Gal 6:17: *"Finally, let no one cause me trouble, for I bear on my body the marks of Jesus."* Each of us will bear scars testifying of our own personal struggle by which we became His.

A fierce conflict is waged in the dressing room as we wrestle to become clothed in our inheritance. The marks that we incur attest to our legitimate sonship. They authenticate us in the spirit realm. They become the distinguishing thread with which the Master Weaver skillfully spins our garment. The marks of Jesus transform us into bold and confident warriors.

The agonizing tension and warfare within our soul as we contend for our inheritance is powerfully described in Song of Songs 5:2-7:

> *I slept but my heart was awake.*
> *Listen! My lover is knocking:*
> *"Open to me, my sister, my darling,*
> *my dove, my flawless one.*
> *My head is drenched with dew,*
> *my hair with the dampness of the night."*
> *I have taken off my robe — must I put it on again?*
> *I have washed my feet — must I soil them again?*
> *My lover thrust his hand through the latch-opening;*
> *my heart began to pound for him.*
> *I arose to open for my lover, and my hands dripped with myrrh,*
> *my fingers with flowing myrrh,*
> *on the handles of the lock.*
> *I opened for my lover,*
> *but my lover had left; he was gone.*
> *My heart sank at his departure.*
> *I looked for him but did not find him.*
> *I called him but he did not answer.*

> *The watchmen found me*
> *as they made their rounds in the city.*
> *They beat me, they bruised me; they took away my cloak,*
> *those watchmen on the walls!*

In this passage the Lord comes to His Beloved. She has progressed to a level of maturity where her heart is now fully awakened and she knows the sound of His knocking. He comes fresh from the night battle. He comes for HER. They have experienced sweet times of love together. In the beginning, with one glance of her eyes, she had stolen His heart. He brought her to the banquet hall and it was there that she fainted with love. He trained her on the summit of Mount Hermon, rejoicing alongside her as she triumphed over the dens of lions and conquered the mountain haunts of the leopards. She is His and tonight He has left the battle and come for her.

But she resists His overtures of love. She is not dressed for battle and this night she will have none of its rigorous demands. Instead she spurns Him. His passion burns for her, and He thrusts His hand through the latch-opening, then turns and leaves. Her heart pounds for Him. Her hands and fingers drip with the bitter sweetness of myrrh as brokenness erupts from her heart. Realizing her foolishness, she runs to open for Him, not knowing He is gone. Her heart sinks and she runs out into the night calling His name.

Tirelessly she searches through the city streets and squares. She walks the darkened alleys. She calls and calls His name. If only she could find Him. Oh! She must find Him! Her silly love, her frivolous quest, attracts the city watchmen. They do not like her being here. They do not know her Lover and have never met Him. They're just doing their job, making their rounds, keeping order and enforcing protocol. They beat her and they bruise her.

AND THEY TAKE AWAY HER CLOAK.

No, no, no, dearly beloved. It is not easy to get this thing on and it is not easy to keep it on. Dreams do not become reality for those who are faint-hearted. Jesus stands in our future and beckons us, *"This way. Come this way. This is the way I long to bring you."* But there are the lion's dens and the mountain haunts of the leopards. As we contend for our inheritance, we will face opposition both from within and from without. We will war with the duplicity of our own heart. We will war with fear. And we will war with the watchmen.

In Genesis 37 we read the story of Jacob's deep love for his son Joseph. We read of the richly ornamented robe that Jacob made for him. But Joseph's brothers hated Joseph because of the robe... because of his dreams... and because of the love that their father lavished on him. They were jealous of him and they stripped the robe from him. Then they sold him into slavery. Sometimes the watchmen are of our own household.

***

Time passes slowly as we trudge from one battlefield to the next in this process of getting our garment on. We have been faithful. We have endured. And then early one morning as we are heading off to our first class on *The Proper Techniques of Sword Polishing*, suddenly, without warning, we catch our self singing. The watchmen stare suspiciously. It is a defining moment. Quietly, the revelation overtakes us. Something has changed. In the midst of this marathon footrace, something has changed. We are not the same.

The warm showers of His cleanness cascade over us and we laugh softly. We feel peace. It is true. The foundations of our heart have been quietly, gradually shifting. We have become softer. We are more content. More and more we find our self lingering at the little white garden table... behind the lattice work... not wanting to leave. He has become our Friend. We have begun to trust Him implicitly and are not nearly as afraid anymore. A new confidence and a new boldness has risen up within us. A new strength has overtaken us. We no longer fall as often. When we do, we don't stay down as long. When we look in the mirror, we catch glimpses of Him.

And oh, yes, you are right. Yes, you are so right. We sing. Sometimes we even hear Him singing over us.

***

During this time I passed through a season when my spiritual compass stood in great jeopardy of demise. The enemy came to torment me about my future and the days ahead. People whom I walked with and trusted in began to rebuke my dreams and to scold me for pursuing them. I began to feel ashamed for even believing in them. My thoughts became ambiguous and distorted and felt as if they were all twisted in knots. One minute I would cry out to the Lord that He could have my dreams. That He was all I wanted. The next minute I felt as though I would betray Him should I fail to contend with all my might for the very thing that I knew in my heart He had created me for and that I knew would bring glory to His name. My garment was under attack.

It is a dastardly evil thing when the enemy comes scheming to abort the purposes of God for our life. Over and over again we will face off with him concerning our destiny. I was ambushed and under siege of confusion and the Lord wonderfully came to me in two separate dreams to shake me from my stupor.

In the first dream that the Lord gave me, I was on my way going somewhere when I came to some type of artery that had to be crossed over. I could clearly see the place where I had to get to waiting on the other side. The sun was shining brightly and it was a very beautiful area with flowers and trees and lush foliage.

A crowd of people was blocking the way through the artery and I had to stop. The only opening was behind a wheelchair that was parked right next to me. I tried to squeeze through but couldn't. The woman in the wheelchair, who was very overweight and unattractive, acknowledged me but would not move. I then felt condemned for wanting to get through and drew back. The crowd then began to move and I followed behind the wheelchair to the area where I was headed. As we arrived on the other side the woman suddenly stepped out of the wheelchair and began walking forward. She was now a very cosmopolitan, sophisticated woman in high-heels and a black and white striped dress.

My dream had one clear, loud message: I'd been had! Whenever we begin to lay hold of our God-ordained destiny, whenever we dare to believe in the dream within our heart and become serious about pursuing it, Satan will oppose us. Even as the sun is shining brightly down upon us and we are bravely navigating the yellow brick road of great faith and confidence, without warning we can suddenly encounter that tight and constricted place wherein there appears to be no way through. And often it is people who block the way.

We must be very wise if we are to keep our compass intact. We must be very, very wise, beloved. The way will be difficult and precarious. Even as we have our eyes fixed upon our destination and are innocently pressing toward the goal, the enemy will appear right beside us, a lie masquerading as truth. If possible, he will cause us to shrink back in confusion and condemnation.

Self-condemnation will always cause us to draw back, for it is only by faith that we can advance. Dear ones, let no man condemn your fervor. Never surrender your faith. Apart from your dreams you will perish. Dream on, dear one. Dream on. Guard your dreams jealously. Be alert. During this time a haunting sadness had come upon me as I had begun to believe that the right thing to do was to put my dreams in a coffin. Deception is a wicked and blasphemous thing. Quite the sophisticated dame, Lady Deception struts and flaunts her black and white stripes. Lies and truth mixed. Darkness and light conjoined.

> STAY UP CLOSE TO THE ONE
> WHO CALLS HIMSELF THE TRUTH.
> STAY UP CLOSE TO THE ONE
> WHO CALLS HIMSELF THE LIGHT.
> STAY UP CLOSE.

In my second dream I was sitting in a restaurant with a friend and two national pastors. These pastors were important men. The atmosphere in the dream was very serious. One of the pastors leaned over and told my friend something about me. My friend agreed that he should share it with me. The pastor turned to me and said that the Lord had shown him that I was living in sin – that I was married to two husbands. Again, in this dream, I felt ashamed and confused. I knew it wasn't true, yet I began to believe it because he said it. I felt strong condemnation and in the dream I went home and began scrubbing and scrubbing my shirt in a desperate attempt to wash out the stain of sin. But all that kept coming out was pure white.

The Lord was amplifying the first message. I had to grow up and become wise enough to resist the wiles of the enemy. I had to become unshakably secure in who I was so that I could quickly recognize and refute false accusation. The games were over. In this dream I had accepted as true something which I knew to be false simply because it was spoken to me by a pastor. It was imperative for my survival and spiritual advancement that my own voice should arise within me to a level playing field with that which I accorded to others, perhaps even most especially to male authority figures. God wanted to break that inappropriate fear of man.

Each of us is responsible to steer our own life. I was wasting precious time at the sink trying and trying to wash out a stain that wasn't there. My deception was so deeply entrenched that God knew the accusation in the dream had to be something I would plainly recognize as a lie when I awoke. Passionately intent upon setting me free, He made the accusation not only blatantly ludicrous, but actually provable. All of us know exactly how many people we are married to!

The father of lies accuses us before our God day and night. His tormenting accusations seek to malign and smear the richly ornamented robe placed upon us by our Father's love. Let us arise in the truth of who we are and cause his fame to be spread abroad throughout all the earth.

You Turned My Mourning into Dancing

In the spring of 2002 I attended a gathering for Women of Strength hosted by Shirley Arnold. It was held at the Secret Place, at that time a leadership restoration and training facility housed on a beautifully rambling and rustic property in Lakeland, Florida. It was a small group made up of all women. On the last evening there was a special time set apart for ministry. As the worship music played, one of the leaders reached for me, pulled me out from the middle of the group, and began to dance with me. "C'mon," she said, "dance with me. I'm the weird one." We danced a long time. Then she began to prophesy over me in very Indian, warlike tongues, kneeling and holding onto my ankles and feet, and then speaking into my abdomen.

> *From this night forward, from this night forward, I say you will no longer feel the bondages in your innermost being. You will no longer feel the bondages when it comes to the area of intimacy that you want to portray before the Father, because He says tonight I have asked you to dance with Me. From this night forward on you will dance with Me, My daughter. You will no longer let the bondages of your past rule thee, but you will be set free indeed to dance before Me. Even because I have invited you to dance. I have taken you in my arms to dance, and I say, And dance you shall. You shall dance in the courts of your King. You shall dance with jubilee, I say, for the spirit of heaviness is being broken off of you tonight. The spirit of bondage is being broken off this heart that has been wounded all these years.*

I was amazed as her words deeply impacted me. For several years we had been attending a church whose worship expressions included dance. At every service there were those who danced. Especially there were two women, trained in ballet, whose movements were very strong and beautiful. I remember during those years being at a retreat where a young husband and wife presented a dance together. They were dressed in boots and army fatigues and danced to a song called *The Lord Is A Warrior.* It had greatly touched my heart.

I began to encounter spiritual dancing more and more. Spending time around it and seeing it so much, it became a very normal thing to me. I would watch and observe and even sometimes want to do it. But I always stayed in my seat.

Now, standing there that night in Lakeland, the Lord's words were like honey to my heart. No one had ever spoken the word dance to me before and it would be over four years until anyone would again. But I carried that word home with me and knew that I was pregnant. As I read over and over what had been spoken to me, I could hear the Lord's passionate invitation. He was asking me, inviting me, even taking me in His arms to dance.

For years I had watched people dance to the Lord and there had even been those few times in my own home that I had danced before Him. But it was not easy to miss His choice of words. He was inviting me to dance *with* Him. I had never danced *with* the Lord. What could that even mean?

I did not know how to dance with the Lord. I didn't know at all what to do. As I asked Him for understanding, I began to remember when I was sixteen and was falling in love with Hollis. Every Friday night there would be a dance held in the school gym. The room would be packed tight. The air was sweaty and heavy with perfume and cologne and the lights would be turned down low. I would get there early and find a chair against the back wall where I would gather with my girlfriends and watch for him. He was handsome and stood taller than the crowd and was easy to spot. At last I would see him come through the door. My heart would explode inside me as he came across the dance floor toward me. Then there was a rush of euphoria as our song would begin to play.

I ran into my closet and put on something pretty. I put some perfume on. I went and got a kitchen chair. I placed the chair at the end of my closet room and sat down in it. I started to giggle. I said,

"Lord, I've never danced with you before. I don't really know how. But I know you've asked me to dance. And I'm saying yes."

Then I sat waiting… Watching for Him… In my heart I imagined Him coming through the door. I watched as He came toward me. A stillness came over me and to my deep surprise, my heart began to race. I stood up and looked into His face as He reached for me and took me in His arms to dance. Tears ran down my cheeks as together we danced and danced, with no one looking on but the angels.

After a long time I sat. Then quietly I began to sing and as I sang and sang there was a new song that began to rise up out of my heart.

> *Well I thought my heart would surely burst*
> *When You walked through that door*
> *It nearly took my breath away*
> *When I saw that smile You wore*
> *You came across that dance floor*
> *And You walked right up to me*
> *And said, "May I have this dance with you?"*
>
> *Well I can't explain the way I felt*
> *When I stepped into Your arms*
> *I knew that I was lovesick*
> *And captured by Your charms*
> *Lord Jesus I will dance with You*
> *Into eternity*
> *Where we'll dance on the streets of gold*

The times of dancing grew. There were long sweet years when the only dance floor we knew was behind closed doors. So many nights we swirled round and round with nothing but the moonlight and the kitchen tile beneath our feet. Little by little our dance began to change. In the beginning there were quiet love songs as we held each other tight. But then a different sound, a new sound, a sound that I loved, began to come out of me. The sound took hold of me and I could not live without it. The dancing became a fiery, intense stomping and what seemed like a tribal war cry began to erupt from within me. It was as the prophetess had said: "He says there lies your victory over ALL things. That is what has kept you, and that is what's gonna continue to keep you is that place where you can just get down and dirty with the Lord, so to speak ..."

After many years, there began to be public times... in Jerusalem, in Odz, Hungary, in Washington D.C., in Rome, in the farming communities and the coastal cities of AmKevina, in Canada. Everywhere I go, my heart listens for the sound. It is rising up in all the nations of the earth. And when I hear it, I dance!

<hr>

In her book *Invitation to Encounter*, Julie Meyer, a worship leader at the Kansas City International House of Prayer since 1999, shares a dream in which the Lord came to her saying, "I want you to meet My friends." He took her by the hand and they began flying around in the sky, doing loop-de-loops like they were in a cartoon. Julie writes:

> *Even though we were extremely high above the ground, I was so aware of not being afraid; I loved just holding His hand and feeling the wind on my face.*
>
> *Suddenly His countenance changed. He set His face intently toward Earth and we started heading directly toward the ground in a head-first dive... I knew He had already decided what He was going to do. He was not going to turn around. I felt horrible dread come over me as we kept descending, even though I was holding His hand.*
>
> *We didn't crash. We exploded right through the ground... I could hear the earth exploding around us as we traveled through rock, water, and burning fire... I felt the earth pounding my body,*

and I could feel my skin burning and tearing. I was in immense pain in my dream... Suddenly we burst through the other side of the Earth. I stood there looking at my body for a moment... My skin was lacerated. My body was weak and aching. I was crying because I was in so much pain. I thought, Surely He sees how badly my skin is wounded and torn... Jesus was aware of my pain, but He made it known that it was not about me. He said to me, "I want you to meet My friends."

He began walking. As I followed Him, I noticed that we were in a very crowded place. I knew it was India. There were little children everywhere who were suffering. I saw some lying on the ground with flies crawling on their skin... I saw beautiful young girls in cages, with whom He continually stood. The Lord calls these seemingly forgotten ones His friends. Not one of them is forgotten in His eyes.

The sadness of what I was seeing, along with the agonizing pain in my body, left me in tears. The Lord came over to look me in the eye. I thought He had finally noticed my pain and was coming to comfort me. Instead, He revealed my self-centered response and invited me to feel His heart: "Until your heart is torn like your flesh is now, you do not know how I feel about My friends."

...I saw children dying, mothers taking their last breath, young girls being sold, and disease spreading. It was more than I could handle. He said again, "Until your heart is torn like your flesh is now, you do not know how I feel about My friends. You do not know Me."

As I looked at the staggering injustice all around, to my surprise, He came near to reveal His secret weapon against it. He whispered, "It is time to dance."

He began a rhythmic, tribal stomp. His perfect feet with their scars of passion were bringing justice by stomping out the injustice done to His friends. He said again, "Until your heart is torn in two, you do not know how I feel about my friends. You do not know Me."

Then He grabbed my hand and we blasted through the center of the earth again… horrible pain of my flesh tearing away from my bones… When we came out on the other side, we were in some kind of clinic that was cold, bleak and unfeeling… I looked around and saw trashcans filled with babies. I could see heads and hands and tiny feet filling can after can. Some were still twitching and staring blankly. Some had burned skin. Others sat there unmoving; there heads were crushed. I could not move or speak when I saw them – I just stood there trembling…

The Lord bent down to be close to His discarded friends. He turned to look up into my eyes and said, "Until your heart is torn like your flesh, you do not know how I feel about My friends. These are My friends."

I felt wounded and exposed – wounded in my body and exposed in my heart. As I stood there sobbing, He got right in my face and said in a low whisper, "It's time to dance." With those perfect feet that tread the high places of the earth, He began dancing and stomping right in the middle of the abortion clinic. It was so powerful.

Each time when I was the most broken and the most undone, He would always say, "It's time to dance; it's time to war. To dance is to war." Then He would stomp with a new rhythm… The Judge was stomping out injustice with His very own feet. The dance was so full of intensity and authority that it seemed He took up all the air in the room.

He said, "Few have joined Me, but just wait until the earth joins me in this dance. I am extending the invitation, but you can only dance when your heart is the most torn and broken."

We went straight through the earth yet again… He led the way down a street, walking with determination… As we walked together, I realized that we were in Israel… He tipped His head at people as if to say hello…He would catch someone's eye… He looked, and their eyes would widen as they realized who He was… I looked over and, for the first time, saw tears running down Jesus' face. I could hear Him sigh, "Oh, Jerusalem… Jerusalem." I wept and the salt of my tears stung the wounds of my flesh, yet I could not stop crying. I crumpled to a heap on the floor, unable to stand under the weight of feeling His heart. He leaned down and whispered, "It is time to dance."

Suddenly we were in front of the Wailing Wall. He started dancing a tribal rhythm against injustice. I could feel the power of this dance. It was heavy and burning.

Jesus said, "A new dance will come out of worship and compassion for the poor of the earth. When your heart is the most broken for the forgotten – for those I call My friends – it is time to dance." [8]

Dearly beloved, He calls. Listen and you will hear the music. He calls to those whose hearts are broken. To those whose flesh is torn and ripped. It is you He calls. Step out of the shadows, dear one, and leave your bondages behind.

The dance floor is open. His arms are waiting. It is time to dance upon injustice!

DANCE THE DANCE OF FREEDOM!
DANCE THE DANCE OF LIBERATION!
DANCE THE DANCE OF JUBILEE!

CHAPTER SEVEN

Just Who IS That Horse on the Cover?

Psalm 68:11 declares that at a strategic time God will give a command, and a company of women who proclaim the good news will defeat His enemies. …Up to the moment of engagement these warring women will have been forced to lie low, hardly noticed, like gray doves on top of dirty sheepfolds. (Ps 68:13) At the appointed time, God will tell these humbled women to rise up and fight.

The restraints that have held women back will be removed. They will hear the word "fight," and fight they will. When they charge into battle, their enemy will be defeated in the most unexpected way. Surprise will be the key element.[9]

A Noise Like That of Chariots

It is the Father's intention that each of us should stand tall, strong, brave and courageous. This is the all-consuming passion of His heart and it is the eternal business which occupies His being. In John 6:39 Jesus says: *"And this is the will of Him who sent me, that I shall lose none of all that He has given me, but raise them up at the last day."* Jesus has been sent and commissioned by His Father to guard, preserve, and keep us. His assignment is to not lose even one of us.

Our Father will not grow tired or weary. He is unyieldingly relentless in His determination that all who come to Him should make it all the way home. Even as He required of His own Son, so He therefore requires that each one of us learn to prevail over the enemy. He has entrusted His Son to be the author of our salvation, to bring us to maturity, to grow us up into Him, and to qualify us for the marriage supper of the Lamb.

Jesus will never leave and He will never forsake even one of His own. Tucking us up close to His heart and feeding us from an underground stream of love, He builds within us an oasis, a refuge, an impenetrable fortification of unshakable security and utter trust. From this place within the interior of our heart He initiates and oversees His Father's work of fashioning us into warriors. The One who calls Himself the Commander of the Lord's army expertly begins to train our hands for battle.

The sound and the beat of the war dance comes differently to each one of us. It violently invades the place of our fear. Many are hearing the anthem of grace being poured out upon us in this hour and are coming forth from captivity. The earth is rumbling with the sound of an army moving into position. It is a sound not heard before in all of time. The sound and the unfolding panorama is foretold by the prophet in Joel 2:2-11.

> *Like dawn spreading across the mountains*
> *a large and mighty army comes,*
> *such as never was of old*
> *nor ever will be in ages to come.*
>
> *Before them fire devours,*
> *behind them a flame blazes.*
> *Before them the land is like the garden of Eden,*
> *behind them, a desert waste – nothing escapes them.*
> *They have the appearance of horses;*
> *they gallop along like cavalry.*
> *With a noise like that of chariots*
> *they leap over the mountaintops,*

like a crackling fire consuming stubble,
like a mighty army drawn up for battle.
At the sight of them, nations are in anguish;
every face turns pale.
They charge like warriors; they scale walls like soldiers.
They all march in line, not swerving from their course.
They do not jostle each other; each marches straight ahead.
They plunge through defenses without breaking ranks.
They rush upon the city; they run along the wall.
They climb into the houses;
like thieves they enter through the windows.

Before them the earth shakes, the sky trembles,
the sun and moon are darkened, and the stars no longer shine.
The Lord thunders at the head of his army;
his forces are beyond number,
and mighty are those who obey his command.

Just as the dawn comes and spreads itself across the mountains while men are sleeping unawares, so does the Lord's army come, large and mighty, it's tribes beyond number. It's ranks consist of those lovers who have yielded to His regimen of training and discipline. Broken, steadfast, and willing in spirit, they are emerging from hiddenness. They are appearing on the mountaintops of the earth, drawn up for battle, singularly focused straight ahead, marching in line, not swerving from their course, not jostling each other, not breaking rank.

Locusts and Wild Honey

The warriors in the passage above are described by Joel as having the appearance of horses. The horse is an animal that symbolizes power and conquest, war and swiftness. The prophet Zechariah was given a night vision of supernatural horsemen sent out by the Lord, commissioned to go throughout the earth patrolling and bringing back report of what they found.

When Jesus first came to earth, He came to lay down His life as a ransom for sinners. He was carried by a lowly donkey colt into the great city of Jerusalem where His journey to the cross found its fulfillment. Yet this One who loves us and has freed us from our sins by His blood is coming once again. This time He will come on the clouds of the sky with power and great glory, and every eye will see Him. There will be no donkey. This time He is coming to judge and make war and He will be riding on a white horse.

The Lord says in Zech 10:3 that "He will care for His flock, the house of Judah, and make them like a proud horse in battle." Just who is that horse on the cover of this book? The horse on the cover is a prophetic picture of the end-time warrior bride. The horse is you.

In the Old Testament book of Job, there is finally a point when Job and his three friends have completely exhausted God's patience. He has listened long enough to their babble and He now chooses to break His lengthy silence. What follows is an interrogating discourse with Job in which God, gloriously holding nothing back, erupts into an indulgent vindication of His own majesty and sovereignty.

Electric in their nature and thundering forth His greatness, the words stand as a rare and holy glimpse into God's invincible pride in Himself. With razor sharpness they silence the tongue of every man. Contained within this eloquent defense is a short passage where God describes the undaunted spirit and prowess of His magnificent creature called the horse.

> *Do you give the horse his strength*
> *or clothe his neck with a flowing mane?*
> *Do you make him leap like a locust,*
> *striking terror with his proud snorting?*
> *He paws fiercely, rejoicing in his strength,*
> *and charges into the fray.*
> HE LAUGHS AT ~~FEAR~~, *afraid of nothing;*
> *he does not shy away from the sword.*

> *The quiver rattles against his side,*
> *along with the flashing spear and lance.*
> *In frenzied excitement he eats up the ground;*
> *he cannot stand still when the trumpet sounds.*
> *At the blast of the trumpet he snorts, "Aha!"*
> *he catches the scent of battle from afar,*
> *the shout of commanders and the battle cry.*
>
> *—Job 39:19-25*

Selah. Selah. Oh, dearly beloved, dearly beloved! Can you feel the ground moving beneath your feet? What an inheritance has been given to us! What a destiny we have been chosen for! We were made to run with Him… to run strong, adorned with power, our neck strained forward and the beauty of our mane flowing in the wind.

God likens His warrior army to locusts leaping with such destructive quickness that everything in their path is devoured. Nothing escapes them. Rev 9:7 makes a similar comparison: *The locusts looked like horses prepared for battle.*

This is a picture of the spirit that we see in the life of John the Baptist who gathered locusts with his bare hands and devoured them. Along with wild honey they were his diet. The rugged prophet in leather and camel's hair refused the soft culinary delights common to men and searched out instead that which grew wild on its own… that which was tended only by the hand of God. As he consumed the whirring locusts his spirit took on their destructive nature and his life was marked by an untiring zeal to confront sin and unrighteousness.

The warrior bride too will feed upon that which grows in the wilderness and she too will be marked by an unflagging zeal to dethrone the prince of darkness. Unabashedly clothed in the Father's love, she is innocently disconcerting, causing great confusion in the enemy camp. She throws back her head and snorts proudly, striking terror in their hearts. She is fiercely undistracted and overjoyed by her strength as she charges into the fray.

SHE LAUGHS AT FEAR, AFRAID OF NOTHING.

Her heart, aflame with the desire to advance God's kingdom and glory over any rival, is consumed with zeal and she cannot stand still when the trumpet sounds. The word stand still is *aman* and it means to be reliable and faithful. Herein is a profound revelation into the heart and spirit of this army that is coming forth. Upon the blasting of the trumpet, the far-away scent of battle, the shout of commanders and the battle cry, the true end-time bride, in the same spirit as the warrior horse, can no longer be relied upon to remain faithful to the parameters of men to keep her in place!! She was made for war. And when the trumpet sounds she will charge.

SHE CANNOT STAND STILL WHEN THE TRUMPET SOUNDS.

In Jdg 7:3 all those of Gideon's men who trembled with fear were released to turn back from battle. In Rev 21:8 those who are cowardly forfeit their inheritance and are given place in the fiery lake of burning sulfur.

The call to arms sounds throughout the land in this hour, promising dire consequences to the cowardly and those who tremble with fear. The sword is extended to you. The lovesick Bridegroom, outstanding among ten thousand, who causes your heart to pound for Him on the dance floor, is the same Lord who thunders at the head of His army. The tenacity to war springs forth from the fires of love. Draw close to Him and the sword will emerge within your heart. With every locust you consume, its size, along with your competence to wield it, will increase.

THE HOUR IS LATE. DAWN APPROACHES. YOU MUST TAKE YOUR POSITION ON THE MOUNTAINTOP.

CHAPTER EIGHT

The Fatal Deathblow

The wedding gown hung quite gracefully on the mannequin, peering out at us from the display window as we parked the car on downtown Eleventh Avenue. My mother clinked her quarters into the parking meter and I followed her as we entered through the large impressive doors that led into Meyer Jonasson's. In all my growing-up years, my visits inside this distinguished clothing store had been only a few. I felt awkward and even a bit frightened.

The gown in the window was brought to the dressing room. It was damaged from long exposure to the harsh rays of the sunlight and the front was deeply yellowed. It was drastically marked down to ten dollars. The gown fit, my mother paid the money, they put it in a box, and we took it home.

We went inside our house and I carried the box with me to my bedroom. All at once my mother was behind me. Reaching out her hand and taking hold of my wrist, she twisted it sharply. Her teeth were clenched. "So help me," she snarled, "if you're pregnant, I'll make you walk down that aisle in black."

Emotional Robbery

The enemy preys upon our vulnerability as little children. In a time when our hearts are young and unprotected, he violates our innocence and stealthily erects his iron castles within our souls, leaving us rent asunder from the loving-kindness of heaven from whence we came, and longing to find our way back.

My life had seemed almost always overshadowed by fear. It is the dominant emotion in all of my memories. I understood that I was to concentrate intently at all times upon doing the right thing, because there was always the looming fear that I could do the wrong thing. I remember vividly an incident from my first-grade year. Mrs. Irwin had taken a short leave from the classroom, with instructions to all of us to remain seated while she was gone, keeping our heads down. My desk was right beside the high, tall window that looked out over the blacktop playground. The hot sun was beating down on me and the time stretched on. Finally, the little girl that was me walked over to the window and tried hard to pull down the big blind. But my small hand lost the cord. The blind madly recoiled and flew off the window. I stood terrified, swallowed up in darkness as yards of fabric engulfed me.

Life was serious. The freedom to laugh seemed slowly stolen from my childhood heart. There were fearful nights when my brother would come to my room and together we would huddle in the dark under my bedspread, comforted and made brave by one another's love. I knew that the next day, and every day after, I must be careful, very careful, to obey all the rules.

As I grew, my birthright in God slipped further and further from me as Satan caused the living waters of my heart to be dried up and my perception of life to become rooted in lies. I worked hard to do everything right, all the while becoming more and more self-righteous. At the same time an escalating anger simmered within me, along with an insatiable hunger for love.

My mother did not encourage conversation. My only assignment was obedience. In his first year of college my brother died and I stepped into my future of being an only child. It was my brother's closest friend who was about to become my husband. "Are you sure you want to marry her?" my mother asked him. "Why, she is the most selfish person on earth. Surely you don't think you can live with her!"

P.S. The gown looked beautiful.

When I gave my life to the Lord, I came to Him just as I was – full of determination to do everything right. But as I walked with Him, and as our relationship grew deeper, I repeatedly found myself up against a rock wall. He was not like others. Love was the only thing He required and I didn't know how to love. It was quite probable that in all my life I had never loved anyone but myself. Yet I wanted more than anything to please Him.

I did not, indeed could not, perceive the length of the journey that stood facing me. Nor could I imagine then the grace and power of the cross that would bring me through. The sincerity of my heart could not be questioned and yet I could not deliver the goods. I labored hard and I cried out and I wept. But progress was minuscule and strong condemnation haunted me as I confronted the gaping hole and inadequacy in my own heart. I battled against raging insecurity and a fearful sense of isolation as I began to feel hopelessly different, ashamed, and defeated. I was convinced that something was wrong with me and that it could never be fixed.

Our Father in heaven watches intently over the life of each of His children. When we draw near to Him, He always draws near to us. All throughout this time, the Lord was building something very solid within me. Over and over He saw my heart and He invested in it. And each time I responded, He invested some more. Unseen and in secret, the Lord was one by one dislodging the stones that had calcified my heart.

In those times when I would sit with Him, waiting upon Him and seeking His face, the warm waters of love were beginning to trickle down over the jagged and bruised landscape deep inside me... ever so slowly at first, and yet pure and clean. Many times my wounded heart fought back, only to be brought to tears as the shadow of the cross reached for me.

As we faced-off with one another during those long years, both the Lord and I remained relentless in our pursuit of wholeness. I found myself longing for the sweet wisdom that accompanied His chastening. And the fear of the Lord began to become my delight.

Decades would pass before the root of bitterness that had poisoned me would be completely pulled out.

The Great Extraction

The estrangement between my mother and me grew worse as my own children grew older. We lived hours apart and things were strained when we were together. I always felt her disapproval. My parents were angry about my relationship with the Lord and angry with my failure as a mother. During our visits I was belittled, cursed, slapped, and at times ordered to leave their home. If I tried to speak, my mother would hold her hands over her ears and scream at me, "Don't you ever speak to me like that in my house!"

During the long night of darkness that settled over our own household, my parents refused to see me. Their letters of condemnation came regularly in the mailbox and my hands would shake with fear and my stomach would recoil in knots as I carried the letters into the house. I knew that if I did not read them I would incur their punishment.

1Cor 13:9 says, *For we know in part...* In my heart I believe deeply that the Holy Spirit would quickly confirm that it is also true that we remember in part. My mother and father both lived inside their own prison of pain - a prison built in part by me. My mother walked through all of these things from her own side of the story – a side that only she can remember and a side that will never be written. She has given me her blessing to tell my side. The story of my mother and me is a love story of two very crippled women who were tenderly and passionately pursued by the stubborn mercy of a

Savior longing to set them free!

❦

My mother had been widowed just a short time when my husband and I made the long winter trip home to get her and bring her back to spend the holidays with all of us. We had all bought little gifts for her and they were waiting for her under our tree. Benjamin, our young seven-year-old grandson, went on the trip with us. We arrived at my mother's cottage in the early evening.

Benjamin and his grandpa staked out their territory in the spare bedroom and happily began to settle into their pajamas. I stayed in the kitchen with my mother while she puttered. Soon Benjamin, having eaten a very early dinner, wandered out hungry for a snack and his great-grandmother offered him an orange. Climbing up on the stool, he ate his orange, and then ran off to rejoin Grandpa. But my mother was upset that Benjamin had been wasteful and had not eaten the orange correctly. She ordered me to call him back to the kitchen and make him eat it properly, which to her included all of the rind.

My stomach began to churn as I stood silently. I felt trapped. It was always this way. I was for peace, but she was for war. "You're not going to do it, are you?" she screamed at me. "You're so high and mighty that you don't have to listen to anyone!"

"Mom, it's alright," I said softly and respectfully. "He hasn't ever been required to eat it that way. It wasn't anything wrong in his mind." I smiled as I cleaned off the counter and I said, "It's just a generational thing."

I went into the bathroom and began to get myself ready for bed. My mother came in behind me, pushed her face into mine, and began screaming again. Again I felt trapped and again I answered her softly, but she began to grab me. All of a sudden rage rose up within me. Hot, ugly rage. I took hold of my mother's neck with both my hands and literally felt dizzy from the dark hatred that began to swirl around me. I stood staring into her face… the face that somehow, even after all these years of tears and earnest prayer, I could not get free from. Then slowly my hands loosened their grip and I let go.

By now Hollis and Benjamin were aware. My mother was eighty years old and very frail. She dropped herself to the floor in the hallway and began gasping for Hollis to help her, screaming frantically that her own daughter was trying to kill her. Hollis did what he could to calm everything but the air was filled with tension. My mother grew extremely cold and stony and ordered us to leave.

The night was late as we carried our suitcases out of the cottage and loaded them back into the car. I tried to go inside again to hold her, to attempt some sense of reconciliation, but her door was locked and she would not respond to my calling. Hollis put the car in reverse, slowly backed out, and turned west onto the lonely, winding mountain road.

When we came to an old dirt pull-off, I asked Hollis to stop. I reached for Benjamin and held him close. I asked if we could go back. Surely we needed to go back. She was all alone and I was frightened for her. But within ourselves we knew it would only make things worse. Something very final had occurred. Her door was closed… perhaps forever.

<hr>

For weeks my dreams tormented me. Night after night I woke up wrestling, my arms wildly flailing the air. We were severed from one another and I was numb with the weight of it. The days dragged by as if all of life had ceased. The sickness of my own heart was like an incurable wound and despair flirted with me as I came face to face with the knowledge that anything so dark and evil could live inside me.

Yet all the time the Lord's arms were holding me tight. Somehow I understood that He had seen this day from afar and now rejoiced to welcome its coming… That He had been preparing me for a long time. O Lord, my God! O Lord, my God! Have mercy on your servant and deliver me!

At last one morning I awoke and knew what I must do. I showered, packed a bag, and gathered together my mother's unopened Christmas gifts. I stood in the kitchen while Hollis prayed with me, sharing his words of wisdom, and blessing me to go. Then I climbed into the van and headed home.

For hours I traveled in silence. Then, turning onto the road that led up over the mountain, I knew it was time. I kept remembering something about Corrie ten Boom, the woman whose family had provided refuge for the Jews in Holland during the Holocaust, and whose story is told in The Hiding Place. As a little girl, Corrie's father had promised her that whenever it was time to board the train, then God would provide her ticket. When she needed it, it would be there. It was time and I needed my ticket.

"Lord Jesus," I prayed, "I'm asking You to give me a love for my mother. Lord Jesus, I don't have any of my own, and I'm asking You to give it to me. I'm about to board the train, Lord. In just a short time, I'll be standing on her porch and I need my ticket. I'm asking You, Lord Jesus, to put Your love for my mother into my heart."

All of a sudden, right there in the van, the words of John 15:12 shot up from deep within me. "My command is this: Love each other as I have loved you." As I have loved you… As I have loved you… As I have loved you… The words rolled over and over in my mind like a powerful cascading waterfall. They were charged with electricity as my spirit man rose up to lay hold of the revelation! The Lord was not asking me to love my mother the way that He loved her. He was asking me to love her as He had loved me.

It was profound. Profound! Yes, yes! Oh, yes, yes! That was a love I knew. Oh, how I knew that love! That was the love that had brought me up out of darkness. That was the love that had carried me when I could not put one foot in front of another. When I had cried out for the grave, when the well within me had run dry, when the hurt and the pain had caused me to lash out against an unseen enemy, that was the love that had put a song in my heart and taught my feet to dance. That was the love, oh, that was the love, that had made me whole again. Tears streamed down my face and my heart overflowed with brokenness. I knew I could give that love to my mother.

That was the love that had the power to heal both of us.

I pulled into town and found a small market where I could refresh myself. Snow was falling and it was bitter cold as I turned down my mother's lane, parked the van, and made my way up her front walkway. The grayish afternoon snow was quickly growing even heavier as I knocked on her door.

When she opened the door and saw me, she turned almost ghostlike as every bit of color drained from her. Shrieking in terror, she slammed the door shut. The winter wind whipped hard over the porch as I lifted my hand and knocked on the door again. There was no response. I continued to knock and knock, yet still there was no response. Through the narrow window I could see her sitting in her kitchen, the light on above her, hunched over her old sewing machine.

I began to call out to her. "Mom, open the door. Open the door." I kept knocking and calling, and calling and knocking. After a very long, long time, she came to the door.

She screamed at me, enraged, through the window. "Go away! Go away! I don't know you. I have no daughter. I have no daughter anymore. Go away!" And she went back to her sewing.

I kept knocking and calling. "Mom, open the door and let me in. Open the door."

Again she came and began screaming, "What do you want? Why did you come? I don't ever want to see you again."

I said, "Mom, it can't be that way. We have to make things right. We belong to each other."

At last she angrily opened the door just enough for me to step inside. "Well I suppose you can stand inside here," she said in an icy voice, refusing to look at me. "I know its cold out there and you've come a long way." And so I stepped just inches inside the door and she backed up, standing several feet away from me.

Love overwhelmed my heart and a soft humility and tenderness settled over me. I stood quietly. My mother began to lash out at me with strong verbal accusations as all the anguish inside her found its target. She carried a lifetime of deep wounds and many of them had come from me. Where the circle began or ended was of no concern. Finally there was quiet and I spoke. Smiling, and joking lightly, I lovingly teased her, "So there's not anything good about me, Mom?" "Oh no!" she spewed viciously. "There's nothing good in you! Nothing! Why even your father knew that!"

Again it was quiet. "Mom," I asked, "would it be alright if I held you?" And stepping toward her, I gathered her in my arms. All of my body began to quiver. "I'm so sorry, Mom. I'm so sorry for all the ways that I've hurt you… All the ways that I've disappointed you as a daughter. I'm sorry that Bobby died and you had to go through that. I'm sorry that Dad died. I'm sorry for all the pain, Mom. I love you." And I held her and could not stop shaking.

My mother was so little. Showing no emotion at all, she stepped back from me, still unable to look at me, and said, "Well… well… why don't you go out and get your suitcase and bring it in. You've traveled a long way. Maybe we can start over again."

I stayed for two days. I never completely stopped shaking and I never stopped quietly crying. She cooked and we ate. She talked and I listened. The atmosphere seemed almost holy and I believe there were angels abiding with us. My mom was not able to ever show any emotion and even struggled to accept her Christmas gifts. But she never once made fun of me or showed any disrespect. Surely something new had been born.

Amazingly, beyond all of this, the work was not yet complete and two years later there came one last unexpected eruption. The

Lord was drilling down, drilling deeper, calling up an even deeper love. The weight of the testing left me spiraling downward until I hit rock bottom and it was there the Lord dealt with me. He reached down from heaven, gripped His mighty hand forcefully around the entire massive root of unforgiveness in my heart, and began violently twisting and pulling on it, determined as He was in His heart to unloose its hold upon me once and for all.

The battle was torrential and the victory required the prayers and love of several trusted friends who came alongside me. It was a prolonged, intense time in which I drew apart to do business with the Lord until, at last, full and complete forgiveness toward my mother was finally released.

An Eternal Bond Restored

There is a death that begins to work in any son or daughter who rejects a parent. Parents have a preserving effect upon their offspring. When a child fails to honor a parent, he cuts himself off from the divine transference of life that flows down through the generations. In a very real sense the child, irrespective of age and aware of it or not, is adrift at sea.

All the while the Father watches while His love contends for the turning of our hearts. Mal 4:5,6 says:

> "*See, I will send you the prophet Elijah before that great and dreadful day of the Lord comes. He will turn the hearts of the fathers to their children, and the hearts of the children to their fathers; or else I will come and strike the land with a curse.*"

My mother moved rapidly into Alzheimer's. But during those few months, as she made her short journey into this final stage of her life, Heaven smiled on us and restored all that had been stolen. It seemed the more her mind receded, the more her heart took flight. We fell in love, saying hello to each other for the very first time. And as she slowly faded further and further away, we said goodbye. I found myself weeping over her life in the night. I had asked of the Lord that He would make everything right for her on this side of eternity, before calling her to Himself, and His marvelous faithfulness supplied our every need.

Somewhere in all of this, while my mom was still able to scuffle about in her walker, there took place a moment that will stand forever isolated on the timeline of my life and of my destiny in God. To my mother, and to others, the incident bore no particular significance, much less eternal weight. But the heart knows its own thirst. And what took place, and the words that my mother spoke, were a drink of cold water from afar.

For a long season of time, years and years, God had been restoring my battered soul bit by bit. Eventually there came a time when I began to enjoy a newfound confidence in who I was. I grew to perceive myself differently and to carry myself differently, and with childlike abandonment, I became aware of a strong stirring of creativity and design that was dancing inside of me. This was new territory for me and one of the places where it began to show up was in my personal clothing style.

So there we were that memorable day... sitting together in her cottage... when my mom began looking at me. Her eyes became fastened on my clothing. Then suddenly, struggling to pull herself up, she began to hobble toward me. So frail and tiny, inch by inch she pushed her walker all the way across the room, until she was as close as she could come to me. Unsteady, and barely able to stand, she reached out her gnarled hand and took hold of my clothing.

She had spent years at her sewing machine and her hands had worked with so many kinds of materials. Now she bent her face down and peered intensely while she turned the tweedy fabric of my clothing over and over, back and forth, between her fingers. "Oh darling," she said, "your clothes are so... so..." and she labored for the right word... "so different," she gasped, out of breath. Thoroughly spent, she began to stumble backward, and I reached out to catch her.

My heart seemed to freeze in time as I instantly recognized what had taken place. Quite unconventional, to be sure, but oh, I knew what it was! The Lord was granting the parental blessing over my life. *Esau…burst out with a loud and bitter cry and said to his father, "Bless me – me too, my father!"* (Gen 27:34) My mother was speaking the parental blessing that had been held back for years.

Perhaps for some it appears all too irregular. But not so, dear reader. You must learn to eat from the table that is set before you. (Ps 23:5) Jesus said, "My sheep listen to My voice" (Jn 10:27). God was bestowing beauty out of ashes. Love had triumphed. Standing as the link between me and all the generations of my bloodline that had gone before, my mother had released the transference of life and grafted me into the covenantal flow of family blessing.

My mother who had birthed me… My mother who had given me life… My mother who had been chosen for me from before the foundations of the world… It was her voice, her words, declaring over my thirsty heart: *I see your gift. I see this outward expression of that which dances on the inside of you. I was drawn to it, attracted to it, and I have even come up close that I might see it better. I have touched it and examined it. And I have this to say concerning it: "It is different." That which lives inside of you is different. That which God has clothed you in is different. It is different from me. It is different from what I have seen on others. It is so, so, so different.*

My mom had blessed me to be different. She had blessed me to be different! She took the very thing that I had been afraid to embrace and lifted it up to a place of honor. The parental blessing comes with great authority and time and time again, in the years to come, her words were destined to silence the voice of the enemy over my life.

"Beloved, Honor your father and your mother, as the Lord your God has commanded you, so that you may live long and that it may go well with you in the land the Lord your God is giving you" (Deut 5:16).

COME, GREAT SPIRIT OF ELIJAH, WE PRAY, AND CAUSE OUR HEARTS TO BE TURNED.

Is this the little girl I carried?
Is this the little boy at play?
I don't remember growing older
when did they?
When did she get to be a beauty?
When did he grow to be this tall?
Wasn't it yesterday when they were small?
Sunrise, Sunset
Sunrise, Sunset
Swiftly flow the days.
Seedlings turn overnight to sunflowers
blossoming even as we gaze
Sunrise, Sunset
Sunrise, Sunset
Swiftly fly the years
One season following another
Laden with happiness and tears

—Fiddler on The Roof

CHAPTER NINE

A River of Liquid Steel

*T*hen David said to Joab and all the people with him,
"Tear your clothes and put on sackcloth and walk in
mourning in front of Abner." King David himself walked
behind the bier. They buried Abner in Hebron and the king
wept aloud at Abner's tomb... Then the king said to his men,
"Do you not realize that a prince and a great man has fallen in
Israel this day? And today, though I am the anointed king, I am
weak (gentle, tender, soft), and these sons of Zeruiah (David's
sister) are too strong (tough, hardened, inflexible) for me.
May the Lord repay the evildoer according to his evil deeds!"
—2 Sam 3:31-32,38-39

Selfless Lovers

In his book *The Thrones of Our Souls* author Paul Keith Davis
shares a revealing spiritual experience that was given to a friend of
his. In this unique prophetic revelation, the Holy Spirit allowed his
friend's eyes to be opened to both the natural and spiritual realms
at the same time.

*He was allowed to observe how the light within Christians
provides a brilliant illumination easily recognized by the
holy and unholy beings in that domain... Furthermore, this*

experience permitted him to see how our emotions and internal qualities produce distinct light and smell easily discerned by both the angels and demons. For instance, if a person is dealing with anger or jealousy those emotions produce a unique color and scent that evil spirits recognize and exploit... Likewise, divine attributes clothe us in the raiment and colors of Heaven and the fragrance of His presence.[10]

The only question that will be asked of us when we stand before God's judgment seat will be: *"Did you learn to love?"* The Lord cannot command love. Love commanded is not love. There will be a time when He demands obedience from the nations, but then the time to prove our love will have passed. All of God's dealings in our lives are His intentional invitation to us to learn to love. Our Father is passionately committed to the removal of everything within our hearts that hinders love. The absence of love in a life emits a strange, foreign color and a foul, putrid smell readily exploited by the spirit beings. Such things will not be permitted to go through the gates into the Holy City. "Nothing impure will ever enter it..." (Rev 21:27).

In the passage above from the book of the prophet Samuel, we are given a tender glimpse into the heart of King David, a man of whom God testified in Acts13:22: "He [God] testified concerning him: 'I have found David son of Jesse a man after my own heart...'" David has received the news of the death of Abner, the military warrior who owned allegiance to the house of Saul and who had commanded Saul's armies against David's armies. King David's heart is overcome with weakness. He is aghast, grieved, undone by the hardness of his own commander, Joab, the one guilty of stabbing Abner and shedding his blood in peacetime as if in battle. (1Kgs 2:5)

The emotional scene in Hebron that day was witnessed by both angels and demons. They were blinded by the light of David's love. And they could smell the intoxicating fragrance of the Lord's presence cloaking him as with broken humility the king of Judah walked behind Abner's bier. David's weeping at the tomb was heard aloud by the people and by his own testimony it was forever recorded of Abner that he was a prince and a great man.

Such tenderness…Such gentleness…A heart moved and brought to tears by the greatness of another life, even the life of one who had been his enemy. Such was the heart that God rejoiced to find in David. Such is the love described in 1Cor 13:5: "…it is not self-seeking…" The Greek *zeteo heautou* means to seek out, to try to obtain, to desire to possess, or to strive for that which concerns the self.

Many years ago I was given a dream in which I was seated in an airplane as it was spectacularly lifting off from a beautiful elevated rocky cliff and heading out over stunningly blue ocean waters that lay drenched in sunlight beneath. I understood in the dream that I was leaving one continent and returning home to my own. As I looked down at the blue water I remembered times that I had been afraid of flying over water, but the pilot of this plane was so strong and confident and was excited and eager for this trip.

The plane was a full-sized aircraft but oddly there were only two rows of two seats each. I sat in the forward aisle seat while two women sat behind me. All at once there were several stewardesses gathered around me. One of the women seated behind me had thrown up and it had gone on the empty seat beside me. I could smell it. Much of it had landed on my left shoulder and collar. I was wearing a crisp, clean white blouse which I had just purchased for ninety dollars.

The stewardesses were giving great attention to the seat beside me as they thoroughly cleaned it. Then they carelessly swiped their same soiled rag down over my blouse in a very perfunctory manner. "Oh!" I said, looking at my blouse and politely smiling. "My blouse… I just bought it."

Upon hearing me, the woman behind me who had thrown up looked at me with a nasty snarl and said, "I'm so sorry, Patty!" leaving me almost taken aback by her unguarded meanness.

Right then the other woman sitting behind me looked up from her book for the first time and with deep sincerity asked me something about the Lord. I wanted to answer her but at the same time felt that I should give attention to the vomit that was covering my blouse. There were three stewardesses nearby who were now involved with other things and were not the least concerned about my blouse.

I asked if there was a restroom where I could wash the blouse out by hand but no one cared or responded. Suddenly, I was genuinely grieved over my concern for the blouse and somewhat convicted I said out loud, "Oh, am I being too demanding?" And then I saw that the woman behind me had gone back to her book and no longer wanted to talk to me.

Jesus is our Pilot as we soar in this spiritual journey toward our destiny. He is excited and quite confident concerning our victory. He is the Alpha and the Omega, the Beginning and the End. To those who are thirsty He gives to drink without cost from the spring of the water of life. Old fears are driven out and are falling away as we are learning to live in His love. We are overcoming and inheriting as He empowers us to shed our cowardice. (Rev 21:6-8)

We walk with Him, dressed in white garments of purity and righteousness, because we have set our hearts on pilgrimage and because we have joyfully endured the trials and the afflictions of love. We have prevailed over the enemy and have refused to shrink back. The favor of the Lord our God rests upon us as He establishes the work of our hands for us. (Psalm 90)

This journey to love is a lonely journey and each heart will make its journey alone. To conquer your fears you must face them alone. There will be those around you [the stewardesses] who will be unmindful of you and oblivious of your journey. There will be others [the woman who vomited] who will vehemently oppose you and cast ridicule upon your pilgrimage. But finally, dear ones, there will be those who will see the whiteness of your garments and will come asking of you, "Where is the way to life?" From these innocent ones the Holy Spirit has concealed the stench and the spew of battle. They sense only the fragrance of Christ.

If we resist God's overtures in His school of love we will forfeit our position in the kingdom. We have not come to a self-serving gospel of salvation. There is no New Testament basis for a Jesus-as-Savior-only believer. No! Rather we have come to a sacrificial gospel of the kingdom.

God's kingdom is the dynamic rule and reign of God. It is an aggressive, bold, confrontational assertion and declaration of God's dominion, authority, and power over the enemy's kingdom (1Cor 15:24-28). His house will be called a house of prayer for all nations and His kingdom is a kingdom whose King is Love and whose law, currency, and weaponry is love. Selfless, fearless love.

God is looking for those who will pay a price for love. He is looking for those who have weaned themselves from their own selfish ambitions...who have brought the clamorings of their own soul to a place of rest until nothing can any longer offend or make them stumble, (Ps119:165). The flame of Yahweh burns within them. Their one consuming passion is to advance God's kingdom and glory over any rival. In all their battles, like John the beloved, they have leaned their head back against the Lord, until now they have become one whom others can lean back against. With uncompromising consecration they have written and signed a non-expiring check made payable to the King of the kingdom for an amount up to and including their life.

Fearless Bondservants

Love is more powerful than fear and love will break the power of fear. Those who have known the deepest bondages of fear will become radical worshippers of the Messianic Emancipator whose origins are from of old, Who came in the darkness of the night and opened the doors of their prison. Their brokenness and their loyalty to Him will cause the angels to weep. *Love is as strong as death and these ones will not shrink from death.* Their love runs as a river of liquid steel.[11]

Such as these does the Lord recognize as those who are his servants, declaring that "If anyone would come after me, he must deny himself and take up his cross and follow me." Of all others He says, I tell you the truth, I don't know you. No disciple of Jesus can compromise or dilute the timeless message of the cross. Jesus died of a broken heart, despised and rejected by men and forsaken even by His Father, because He was not willing to go to heaven without us. "He endured the cross, scorning its shame... " And so, dear ones, must those who follow Him.[12]

The cross stands naked, stark, and raw, an instrument of death and an affront to all the high-mindedness of self-love. Those who have felt its nails recoil from any pretense of glamorizing it. And many of those who have never felt them nonetheless perilously imagine themselves to be in the company of those who know its resurrection power. But the power of the cross springs from one thing alone - death.

Human wisdom will empty the cross of its power. Many live as enemies of the cross, shunning its offense, and doing whatever they must to avoid being persecuted for it. Refusing to see him who is invisible, refusing to hear His cry of love, and feeding only themselves, they seek to keep their own lives while all the time losing them to their own prison of fear.[13]

Beloved, we must not be deceived. Fear is sin. At its core, fear is a stubborn refusal to trust the goodness of God and to rest in His unchanging power. Trust is the distinguishing characteristic of a believer. Dan 6:23 says: "And when Daniel was lifted from the [lion's] den, no wound was found on him, because he had trusted in his God." No matter the turbulence, no matter the fire, the Lord will always supply His child a firm place for their feet to stand upon. His love will guard, protect, and deliver them even as He is performing

His deep inner work of childlike trust in their heart.

Always, always, the purpose of the cross is to birth an opening in order that the freshness of resurrection life can come forth. The words below were prophetically spoken over me during a time when, having emerged from a very long season of persevering, I seemed now to be standing on the threshold of taking possession of my destiny. These words are rich with the overwhelming confidence of our God and the reason why He is so extravagantly worthy of our trust.

> *For the Lord would say Daughter even know that I'm even causing trust to be restored within your heart says the Lord. And the Lord would say you would have even walked through some situations even in past years where there would have been broken trust with people and the Lord would say it would have even brought a great wounding to your heart. But the Lord would say that even know this day the Lord would say that I'm even causing your trust in me to be re-instilled in different ways says the Lord. And the Lord would say that know that as you hope in me surely you will not be disappointed says God. [Isa 49:23] And the Lord would say that I'm beginning to even stir vision within your heart afresh and anew. And the Lord would say there would have even been that season of time that you would have walked through and it would have even seemed like every dream and every vision would have been crushed for a season but the Lord would say that know that I'm even setting my hand to your life in this season of time says the Lord and the Lord would say that I'm bringing you through and I'm bringing you forward even into a destiny and a purpose says God… And the Lord would say that know that there's even been some challenges of fear that have warred against you, but the Lord would say that I'm even coming to break the power of fear. And the Lord would say that even in some night seasons the Lord would say the enemy would have come to torment you even in some*

> *areas about the days ahead and what to expect. But the Lord*
> *would say that I'm destroying even the power of the torment*
> *and the Lord would say that I'm even releasing you to expect*
> *good things to happen. And the Lord would say that know*
> *even as I begin to open some new doors of relationship to you*
> *the Lord would say you're gonna begin to step through those*
> *doors and the Lord would say that you're gonna find that*
> *there's gonna be trust established once again within your heart*
> *not only with me but with people on a new level says God.*

We must drink deeply from these words. Our Lord stands as a God of restoration. He is not a God afar off. He is grieved when our trust suffers brokenness. He shares the great wounding of our hearts and comes to renew us. Seeing His dreams and visions for our lives lying crushed by the side of the road, "...the Lord stirs up His zeal like a warrior, raises the battle cry with a shout, and comes in the spirit of triumph" (Isa 42:13) to break the power of fear that has warred against us. Ferociously He scales our Mount Everest and hoists our flag of victory. Then He calls out valiantly to us from atop the hill of our future and beckons our revived hearts to believe once more.

Once again we hear the angels singing our song. Once again He leans close and whispers to us of destiny and purpose, while we catch the fragrance of wedding feast wine on His breath. The distant rhythm of drums overtakes our heart and our gladdened feet begin to search for the dance floor. Once again we just know good things are going to happen.

Fear will blind our vision. But as we walk in faith that He is with us, we will always see the way to go. Less and less we will trust our self and more and more we will put our confidence in Him. Our heart is steadfast, trusting in the Lord. Our heart is secure, we will have no fear (Ps 112:7, 8). Unbound and liberated, in love we will go into the end-time harvest to liberate others.

Come now. You must return to the little white garden table and the two small chairs. Remember, beloved… in the kitchen… set apart from the work area… enclosed in beautiful lattice work. You must go there now. As you linger there with Him, you will find yourself once again in the upstairs room. Do not hurry it. These things beg time, dear one. Ahhhh, there now. Yes, yes. Do you see it? The dragon… The great dragon lies dead in the corner. You slew him. Now go quickly to the closet and open it wide. Destiny awaits you and you will need your garment.

IT'S TIME TO PUT YOUR GOWN ON, BABY!

HE HAS FREED YOU
FROM YOUR CHAINS!
—PS. 116:16

Send me into the darkness
I'll shine my light
Let me be as an arrow
Piercing the night
Let me serve living water to hearts that are dry
Send me into the darkness
I'll shine my light

Let me stand on the mountain
Announcing your peace
Let me tear down the strongholds
Proclaiming release
Let me tear off the shackles that men may go free
Send me into the darkness
I'll shine my light

Endnotes

[1] Ruth Bell Graham, <u>Prodigals and Those Who Love Them</u> (Colorado Springs, CO: Focus on the Family, 1991), 148.

[2] Michal Ann Goll, <u>Dream Language</u> (Shippensburg, PA: Destiny Image, 2006), 92.

[3] Don Potter, <u>Prisoner</u>, Potterhausmusic@aol.com.

[4] Gregory R. Reid, <u>Nobody's Angel</u> (United States: Xulon Press, 2005), p. v.

[5] Stephen Hill, <u>Time to Weep</u> (Orlando, FL: Creation House, 1997), 83-84.

[6] <u>Hebrew Greek Study Bible, NIV</u> (Chatanooga, TN: AMG Publishers, 1996), Eph 2:2, Jn 14:30, Rev 2:13, Isa 14:13-15, Ezek 28:12-17, Jn 10:10.

[7] Michael L. Brown, <u>Our Hands Are Stained With Blood</u> (Shippensburg, PA: Destiny Image, 1992), 112-113.

[8] Julie Meyer, <u>Invitation To Encounter</u> (Kansas City, MO: Forerunner Books, 2008), 97-103.

[9] Ed Silvoso, <u>Women God's Secret Weapon</u> (Ventura, CA: Regal Books, 2001), 17-18, 21.

[10] Paul Keith Davis, <u>The Thrones Of Our Souls</u> (Vancouver, WA: Miracle Printers, 2002), 83.

[11] <u>Hebrew Greek Study Bible, NIV</u> (Chatanooga, TN.: AMG Publishers, 1996), Mic 5:2, Song of Songs 8:6, Rev 12:11.

[12] Ibid., Mt 16:24, Mt 25:12, Isa 53:3, Mt 27:46, Heb 12:2.

[13] Ibid., Mt 7:21, 1Cor1:17,18, Phil 3:18, Heb 11:27, Jude 12, Gal 5:11, 6:12-24, Lk 17:33.

www.ingramcontent.com/pod-product-compliance
Lightning Source LLC
Chambersburg PA
CBHW032011040426
42448CB00006B/577